THE COMPLETE BOOK OF
MARTIAL ARTS

THE COMPLETE BOOK OF
MARTIAL ARTS

David Mitchell

GALLERY BOOKS
An Imprint of W. H. Smith Publishers Inc.
112 Madison Avenue
New York City 10016

I dedicate this book to my wife, Paula, who is more a martial artist than a great many older and ostensibly better qualified persons than she. These are not the gushing words of a husband; rather they are the views of a martial artist who has been lucky enough to meet the world's leading exponents in the various disciplines. With only two weeks pre-training, she took on the world's top competitive karate women athletes in Taipei, Taiwan, during October 1982 and came fourth, a mere half point behind the third placing. She was also one of Britain's two female European qualified refereeing officials and has been invited to train under some of Japan's leading karate teachers.

Only one thing has prevented her from doing better, and that is her love for all the martial arts and her desire to see them prosper. Accordingly she has given up her competitive prospects to devote herself full-time to administering those same arts. This is a thankless but essential job, and typical of her martial art spirit, she has succeeded.

With respect,

David L. Mitchell
London 1989

First published in 1989 by
The Hamlyn Publishing Group Limited
a division of
Octopus Publishing Group
Michelin House
81 Fulham Road
London SW3 6RB

This edition published in 1989 by Gallery Books
An imprint of WH Smith Publishers Inc
112 Madison Avenue
New York, New York 10016

Copyright © The Hamlyn Publishing Group Limited 1989

ISBN 0 8317 5825 2

Printed by Mandarin Offset, Hong Kong

ACKNOWLEDGEMENTS

I am delighted to acknowledge the substantial contributions made to the photographic sessions by the following:

Robert Clark directed the technical content of the full contact, jiu jitsu and ninjutsu sessions. Frank Perry provided the use of his excellent gymnasium.

The following demonstrated their martial arts: Ron Sergiew: taekwondo; Simon Lau: wing chun kung fu; Brian Eustace: taiho jutsu, aikido and judo; P Kim: hapkido; Terry Holt: iaido, iaijutsu and kendo; Tony Leung: shaolin five animal styles; Jifu Huang and his daughters: tai chi chuan; Mike Cundy: kyudo; Joe Tierney: karate; student of M K Loke: tang soo do; John Ryan: Thai boxing.

PHOTOGRAPHY

Special photography by **Martin Sellars**
All other photographs reproduced with the permission of the following:
Action Plus/Richard Francis 71, Tony Henshaw 70; Allsport 113, John Gichigi 3, 55, 72, 74, Jean-Marc Loubat/Vandystadt 69, 106 top; Colorsport 7, 20-1, 123, 124, 132, 138, Sipa 139 top and bottom, 140-1, Sipa/Jean Padi 164-5; Sylvio Dokov 13, 29 right, 34 right, 56-7, 58-9, 83, 86 right, 99 bottom, 107 top and bottom, 111, 143, 149, 160-1; Split Second/Leo Mason 75 top; Sporting Pictures 54, 80-1, 133 top, 134, 147, 159; Bob Thomas 43, 142

CONTENTS

TAKE CARE

**Martial Arts' techniques described in this book are
potentially dangerous, the more so if performed unsupervised.
Practise only under the guidance of a qualified coach
or instructor. The author and the publisher cannot accept
responsibility for any injury resulting from practising
the moves described in this book.**

MARTIAL ARTS PHILOSOPHY

The term martial art is applied to a great many activities, some of which have no real military connection, so it is a good idea to begin this book with a clear understanding of what exactly is meant by the term. Strictly speaking, a martial art is a collection of techniques used in waging war. Typically these involve using weapons of one kind or another.

The word 'art' is perhaps a little misleading: it needs no great skill to aim and fire a rifle. The skill comes in selecting and hitting targets, and in maintaining effective fire. The martial art of using a rifle will therefore include these elements and also how to maintain the rifle and ammunition.

Human beings are gregarious, living in tribes and identifying with strong symbols of power. In human societies those who are more effective acquisitors gain a greater share of available resources.

When a community grows beyond the resources available to feed and shelter it, it must expand or decline. When the aspirations and greed of the ruling party cannot be satisfied within the community, their needs must be pursued outside. In both cases, neighbouring resources are plundered. Small agrarian communities are invaded by larger and more aggressive neighbours but equally aggressive neighbours will not yield readily and war develops.

There are two ways of fighting a war: with highly trained professional soldiers supported by the rest of the population or with a few professional warriors leading an army. When the weapons of warfare allow hand-to-hand fighting, a professional warrior is more effective than many conscripts but in times of frequent wars such warriors are killed faster than replacements can be trained, so conscription must be used to bolster manpower.

THE DEVELOPMENT OF MARTIAL TRADITIONS

Around the 15th century firearms became generally available and, unlike the sword, could be used effectively with the minimum of training. For a brief period the old and new co-existed but finally the new martial ways proved more efficient. This introduced a great levelling in martial art practice and meant that a greater number of people could become effective warriors.

When two similarly equipped armies meet, the outcome is decided by a number of factors. The first is strategy: taking up positions and putting the enemy at a disadvantage. Pre-emptive strikes are one way of achieving this.

The second factor is the valour of the warriors. When deployed wisely, fearless and aggressive warriors can gain the initiative more easily than fearful or dispirited opponents. The third factor is the support facilities and relative sizes of the two armies. The bravest and most resourceful of armies need food and equipment. The weakest of armies will triumph if it has overwhelming numbers. Larger nations can afford to expend their manpower wastefully.

Whereas the West usually discarded weapons when they became obsolete, the East has kept them on; for though they may no longer be used on the battlefield, the martial mind they generate remains vital. Some of these traditions are very old, with a written history extending back more than 500 years. There are no doubt still older systems but these have not been recorded, or their earlier existence has been lost. Each tradition was founded through what might be called a mystical revelation and we need only look back to the early parts of the 20th century when a student of aiki-jui jitsu named Morihei Ueshiba experienced a vision of harmony which led him to found the martial art of aikido.

Older traditions have persisted because new developments have been constantly added, until the central core of teaching is overlaid with many layers. The martial art of jiu jitsu, for example, first originated as a way of grappling between armoured warriors and when armour was phased out, the art changed to meet the new situation. This illustrates the important point that martial art traditions are evolving. Attempts to petrify things as they are deny the abilities of present day masters and lead to discontent.

Interestingly, the adjective traditional is often applied to martial arts which are less than 50 years old! It is certainly true that their predecessors go back further but generally there

Nocking the arrow

is a distinctive point, at which it can be said that a new martial art was founded.

THE PHILOSOPHY OF MARTIAL ART

Though the sword might be made obsolete, the martial mind that training with it engendered was not. While the West laid greater and greater emphasis on new weapons, the East never forgot the need to train people to use new technology in an effective way.

People everywhere have a deeply rooted instinct for self-protection which makes them evaluate the odds for personal survival in any life or death encounter. If the urge for self-protection is diminished, however, a combatant becomes unafraid of death and fights without fear. Stories abound about old or weak people fighting off stronger attackers by acting without fear and with total commitment. The importance of mental attitude in producing an effective warrior cannot be over-emphasised and it is convenient at this point to consider some words from the 18th century Hagakure Bushido of Yamamoto Tsunetomo.

Bushido, I have found, lies in dying. When confronted with two alternatives, life and death, one is to choose death without hesitation . . .

A man of great valour does not think of the outcome of the fight; he fervently plunges right into the jaws of death . . .

Bushido means to struggle desperately in the jaws of death . . . even dozens of men find it difficult to kill only one samurai in this frantic state.

A European holding these views would be considered insane, a fanatic, and yet they were wholly comprehensible to mid-20th-century Japanese! A thousand years of military tradition taught that the personality was a temporary alliance of wants and desires, and that life itself was no more than an illusion. One could aspire to no greater heights than to die gloriously in the service of the Emperor.

It is perhaps understandable that Westerners came to attribute superhuman feats of fighting ability to the Japanese and their martial arts, when in fact these systems were of minor importance compared with the power of their philosophy. This misunderstanding has persisted to the present day and there are millions of people in more than a hundred countries all practising techniques which they hope will make them into fearless and invincible suburban warriors. Sadly, without an understanding of the true principles of oriental martial

arts practice, these will at best become mere masters of technique. It is often said that a coward who practises the martial arts becomes a coward equipped with martial art techniques.

MARTIAL ARTS AND COMBAT SPORTS

Archery was practised in both the Far East and the West. In Japan it is still called a martial art but in Britain it is now a sport, and not a martial art. Japanese archery clubs do not exist for the purpose of winning prizes. The practitioner of kyudo is concerned only with the cultivation of a martial arts mind. If the arrow hits the bulls-eye, all well and good but if not, it does not matter.

The founder of Japanese karate, Funakoshi Gichin, saw his martial art as a vehicle for training the mind and body. He opposed the introduction of sporting competition because he correctly foresaw that it would lead to cultivation of the individual.

Modern martial art competition is no different from any other competition, with athletes and spectators alike shouting and screaming for their team-mates. At first the Japanese founders of karate were bemused by this demonstration but with the passage of time, they too no longer sit impassively.

TRAINING

Practising the martial arts requires a certain level of fitness. This may pose no problem for young and active students but older novices should start off gradually, increasing the pace of training as fitness develops. The body's level of fitness varies according to the demands put on it. Students who are also, say, dancers will find no problem with hard martial art training because dancing makes them fit enough, but those with a sedentary job will not be fit enough to launch pell-mell into martial art training.

NOVICE TRAINING

Suppose you are not fit when you begin training. Most martial art practice takes place in mixed-ability classes, so the pace of training is pitched for the majority of students. As a new student you may find yourself pushed beyond your ability to keep up and within a short time, no longer enjoy the training. You can either soldier on through successive training sessions until your level of fitness increases to accommodate training load, or take up a supplementary fitness programme.

It is important to realise that you learn best when you are not over-taxed, so the sooner you become fit, the sooner you can get down to the serious business of learning technique.

A regular daily session that maintains a heart rate of around 140 beats per minute for a full 20 minutes will soon improve your fitness. An unfit novice may not be able to last 20 minutes in which case he should work up to the full period.

Running, jogging, cycling or swimming etc. all work the heart, the lungs, the circulation and the muscles, and after a fortnight or so of daily exercise, will improve your fitness sufficiently to make martial art practice more enjoyable. Thereafter, fitness sessions twice or three times a week, in addition to martial art training, will be all that is needed.

TRAINING FOR COMPETITION

You may want to enter competitions or go in for arduous grading examinations. If so, you will need to train to a higher level of endurance.

This is best achieved by sessions of intense practice in the techniques to be improved, in which students work against the clock, performing as many full-power techniques as they can within a set time, alternated with periods of active rest. By this means the body learns how to cope more quickly with fatigue generated through hard training.

Different martial arts work different muscle groups and until your body adapts, you will inevitably have sore and stiff muscles. You may still be a little stiff at the next session, but within a few minutes, muscle aches will ease as fatigue products are washed out by the increased blood supply resulting from exercising.

STRENGTH TRAINING

It may be that your techniques require more power to make them effective. Power derives from speed and strength, both of which can be

Special training drills are used to improve power

Impact-based martial arts require considerable flexibility at the hip joint for the correct performance of high kicks

improved by special drills. However, speed can only be increased so far, after which all subsequent power improvements must be gained by increasing muscle strength. Strength training must be specific to the martial art, so that sumo wrestlers will improve by heaving man-masses around, whereas someone who wants to punch more powerfully will use only the lightest weights and move them very quickly. Speed training is accomplished by executing the movement to be trained as quickly as possible.

FLEXIBILITY TRAINING

Flexibility at the joints — especially of the hips and spine — is a second limiting factor. Here, unfortunately, martial art training is not helpful and the novice with poor hips will take a great deal of time to improve unless he does an additional flexibility programme. The range of movement at a joint is practically determined by the muscles acting through it and if these muscles are short and tight the joint will be restricted. If they can be made to relax the joint will extend further. Flexibility training consists of no more than making relevant muscles relax.

A common problem in the im-pact-based martial arts is relaxing the thigh adductors sufficiently, so the knee can be raised to the side of the body. This movement is the key to successful kicks. There are many exercises for hip flexibility to choose from but the following is one of the most efficient. Before trying it, students must be aware that they should treat this and all subsequent flexibility drills with respect. They begin with a short session containing a few repetitions and increase loadings as fitness improves.

Lie on your back, with the entire length of the backs of your legs pressed against a wall. Separate your legs, moving them gently down as far as you comfortably can and hold them there for 30 seconds or so, before raising them both a short distance, and holding at the new position for another 30 seconds. Finally relax them and allow them to sink again. This time they should open further because the previous period of tension encouraged the adductors to relax more.

This method is highly effective and its principles can be adapted to whichever muscle groups need stretching. The sequence is stretching the muscles for 30 seconds, contracting them for 30 seconds against resistance and stretching them again.

All stretching exercises should be performed when your body is warmed up. Do them until it begins

▼ **Flexibility training**
1 *Rest your heel on your partner's shoulder*

2 *Lower your head to your knee and be sure to keep your leg straight*

▼ **Flexibility training**
1 *Rest your heel on your partner's shoulder*

2 *Lower your head to your knee and be sure to keep your leg straight*

▶ **Flexibility training**
Allow your legs to separate under their own weight. Then lift them against gravity, before allowing them to open again

to feel uncomfortable, then stop. Ignoring pain can lead to injury and a set-back for the programme. The muscle to be stretched must be relaxed and this can only be achieved by gentle, non-jerky movements.

WARM-UP AND COOL DOWN

The purpose of warm-up is to prepare the body for the demands of training. This is achieved by taking it through a series of exercises which gradually increase in intensity. The exercises chosen must suit the activity to be covered in training proper. The length of warm-up will depend on the time available for the lesson and it should be just long enough to ready all relevant parts of the body,

but neither so prolonged nor so intense as to tire them out.

Although your central body temperature remains constant, temperature in your limbs varies according to external conditions. Muscles are bags of semi-fluid tissue which stiffen slightly when cold, making them difficult to stretch and produce full power. A warm-up session raises temperature in the muscles, loosening them up and making them more amenable to stretching. Warm-up also gradually

increases the rate of heart-beat from its resting level to that needed for training, which is less traumatic than simply plunging into intensive training.

The best general martial arts warm-up is to perform the techniques to be covered in the lesson at a gradually increasing intensity.

It is equally important to cool down after training. Working muscles act as fluid pumps, moving large quantities of oxygen in and waste out. If you stop training

Flexibility training
1 *Twist your hips to the side and bring your forehead to your knee*

2 *Drop your head to the knee of your supporting leg*

abruptly, the blood supply to your limbs quickly falls and fatigue products are trapped there. For this reason, training should slow down gradually to give time for the wastes to be pumped out.

TRAINING AND HEALTH

Correct martial art training benefits the health of most people. However, there are some conditions or situations in which training has to be modified, or perhaps even abandoned. Novices leading a sedentary life and aged over 40 should train at an intensity they feel comfortable with. It makes sense to have a medical before joining a course.

Heart conditions may actually benefit from training, provided that a doctor has cleared participation and that the sufferer can set his own pace. Asthmatics too will benefit, though they must take their medication into the training hall. Diabetics should have supplies of sugary drinks on hand and must alert the coach to their condition. Epileptics may also train if the floor is soft, and must tell the coach about their condition.

Haemophiliacs should not study the martial arts because merely practising the movements may be sufficient to cause bleeding into the joints. It might be possible to train in the internal forms such as tai chi chuan, but medical advice must be sought beforehand.

Physically disadvantaged people will find great fulfilment in martial art practice. For example, blind people practise jiu jitsu and aikido – and there is no reason why they should not do extremely well at such arts as wing chun kuen kung fu. These various arts all concentrate on the feel of an opponent's state of strength and alertness. Wheelchair-bound martial artists can practise locks, holds and weapon routines.

Children enjoy martial art practice and through it, they learn discipline and respect for themselves, and for other students. It is, however, essential that they are correctly coached and taught only those techniques which are appropriate to their skill and sense of social responsibility.

DEVELOPING FORCE

There are two types of martial art today. The first involves weapons, and is practised by a very small minority of martial artists. Kendo and kyudo are both examples of this type, though the former does contain some elements of grappling. Chinese systems usually include some weapon use, in many cases as training aids for wrist flexibility and power development. Korean martial arts involve almost

The fist is a natural body weapon because it can be accelerated strongly

no weapons work, while Okinawan systems use covert weapons.

A weapon makes it possible for a relatively weak person to inflict serious injury, assuming that the user has enough strength and dexterity to wield the weapon effectively. Even without a weapon there are techniques which maximise natural resources. Power can be projected so a strike becomes more powerful; leverage can be applied so strength is no longer an absolute determining factor; the body's natural weapons can be trained until they can inflict injury without themselves being damaged and an opponent's own force can be used against him, so his very strength becomes a disadvantage.

▼ *It doesn't matter if you are standing on one leg; it is still possible to generate force*

Long-hand boxing
1 *Begin from a fighting stance with your hips facing three-quarters on*

2 *Push down with your rear foot and turn your hips to the front*

3 *Allow torsion to build in your spine, then allow your shoulders to swing forward. Withdraw your leading fist and begin the punch*

4 *Project your weight forward as your punching arm thrusts out to its full extension*

PROJECTING FORCE

Acceleration

The faster an object travels, the greater the force it generates. If this force is then released in an instant, it can be devastating. Your fists, feet, elbows and knees are all natural body weapons because they can be accelerated. There are limits to the amount of impact force which can be generated, one being the maximum acceleration that your body can produce in a limb. Once this is reached, other resources must be harnessed.

Strength

Power is the product of speed and strength, so it follows that a strike can deliver more impact if the muscles which power it are made stronger. Fortunately muscular strength is relatively easy to increase by simple body weight exercises.

Absorbing recoil

The third requirement of projecting power is to absorb recoil produced by impact. If a fist is accelerating hard enough, it will have enough energy to counter recoil. A great deal is said about the need to adopt a stable stance but this is generally the least important element in absorbing recoil. Having said that, no-one ever delivered an effective strike while falling off balance! Many people confuse the recoil

effects of a high velocity strike with the force needed to overcome inertia. They wrongly use the analogy of pushing a car to justify the value of stances.

As long as your limb is accelerating as it impacts, and your centre of gravity is moving – even slightly – behind the blow, you are doing all you can to counter recoil. It doesn't matter if you are standing on one leg: the impact force will be the same. Martial artists raised on long forward stances may dispute this but they need only look at the impact developed by those using horse stances, in which there is no fore and aft bracing.

POWER PROJECTION SYSTEMS

Some martial arts use training aids such as inner tubes to strengthen their strikes but all this does is to teach how to punch against the resistance of an inner tube! Such ill-conceived ideas are misleading: the technique feels powerful, so

Martial arts based on the Chinese long-hand boxing systems use the full length of the extended arm to generate maximum force

karate, taekwondo, tang soo do and Thai boxing. In all these the punch accelerates from a bent arm to an almost straight one. The forearm may also rotate from being palm upwards to palm downwards and the fist is pulled tight on impact, not before, which would slow arm extension.

A basic reverse punch is a useful model in which to see the various components of long-hand boxing operate. Typically the punch begins from a middle to long forward stance, with your back knee slightly bent and your hips turned 45 degrees away from facing directly forward. For the purposes of this description a left stance is assumed, with your left fist and leg leading.

The first element in the long-hand punch is turning your hips, so your right hip is brought forward and your right knee straightens fully. As this is happening your shoulders remain still, so a twisting stress is set up in the powerful muscles that support your spine. As your hips

therefore it is judged to be powerful! Unfortunately this is rarely the case. A leading exponent of one martial art has identified the most effective strikes as those which are thrown haphazardly and without skill. What does this suggest?

A punch that travels a short distance to the target is less easy to block than one using the full length of the arm. This understanding has led to the development of two separate systems for power projection, long-hand and short-hand boxing.

Long-hand boxing

Long-hand boxing gave rise to such as the *hung gar* styles of kung fu,

DEVELOPING FORCE

Power-generation in short-hand boxing forms is by a shrugging action of the shoulders and a powerful spasm of the fist and forearm

turn square-on, your left fist is strongly withdrawn, which sets up a swinging action in your shoulders, and an equal and opposite extension of your right fist.

Strange as it may sound, your right fist is powered in part by your withdrawing left fist and both arms move in perfect synchrony. As your punching elbow straightens, your weight is shifted forwards slightly. This is important for countering the effects of recoil. As your left fist reaches your hip, your right arm is virtually completely straightened and both forearms rotate simultaneously, the right turning palm-downwards and the left palm-upwards. Your whole body tightens spasmodically at the point of imagined impact then immediately relaxes once more.

On completion of the punch your shoulders are lowered, with your right side leading slightly. Your right arm is straight and the bones of your forearm have rotated so your elbow joint is locked. From your shoulder to your index and middle knuckles is one straight line. Your hips are facing the front and your right knee is locked. Both feet are planted firmly and your forward movement has positioned your left knee above the toes of your left foot. Your punching fist has not passed beyond an imagined line extending up from your left shin. This is important to classical notions of stability, since if your fist went beyond the line, the ability to absorb recoil would be reduced.

Power development has come from synchronised combination of:

- a twisting action of the hips which loads the spine with power

- a swinging action of the shoulders which uses the power stored in the stretched spinal muscles

- a pulling back of the leading hand to accelerate shoulder action

- a forward shift of the centre of gravity to develop momentum

- a twisting action of the fists to increase penetration

- a spasm action of the muscles to produce a jarring impact.

Short-hand boxing

Compare this with a short-hand punch such as in the southern Chinese system called *wing chun* *kuen*. This system gained a certain degree of fame from claims made about its one-inch punch, which was said to be capable of delivering a strong impact. How can enough acceleration be gained in such a short distance?

The delivery stance for the punch is quite high, with feet in line and hips facing forward. There is absolutely no hip action. Your arms are held well forward in the projected centre-line of your body, with elbows only slightly bent and hands open. Your fist is thrown at the target by a slight shrugging action of the shoulders and straightening the elbow. As your knuckles brush the target your hand immediately snaps closed and your fist tightens convulsively. It relaxes again immediately after impact and the natural springiness of your arm

Tai chi chuan uses a flowing, relaxed action to generate a surprising amount of power

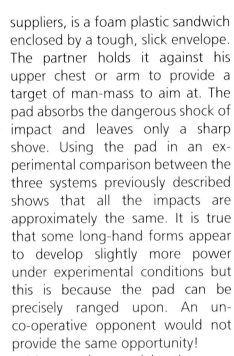

▼ *An impact pad allows you to generate considerable impact force without harming your partner*

muscles provides a fast snap-back.

Your fist does not rotate on impact, but strikes home with the thumb uppermost, making contact with the lower three knuckles. Only the forearm muscles tense on impact, leaving your shoulder relaxed. Actually, this is quite hard to do and requires special training. One training drill uses a long pole, gripped at one end and then swung violently. The action of abruptly stopping the swing produces the arm-tension required by the punch.

Your fist is thrown at the target, rather than being thrust out. Your upper body, shoulder and arm are all completely relaxed and the spasm is strictly confined to the forearm of the punching fist.

External and internal

Both the preceding systems use some degree of obvious muscle spasm in generating power and so they are said to be 'hard', or 'external'. Compare this with systems in which the punch is thrown without any muscle spasm at all. It is hard to see how this could be effective, yet it is! *Tai chi chuan* ('great ultimate fist') is performed in a slow, flowing manner and is often described as 'the old men's martial art'. Those who do so have probably not seen it performed at speed.

The very absence of hard muscular contraction leads to extremely fast movements which, together with the momentum generated, develop a surprising impact.

A training aid known as an impact pad, available from martial arts

suppliers, is a foam plastic sandwich enclosed by a tough, slick envelope. The partner holds it against his upper chest or arm to provide a target of man-mass to aim at. The pad absorbs the dangerous shock of impact and leaves only a sharp shove. Using the pad in an experimental comparison between the three systems previously described shows that all the impacts are approximately the same. It is true that some long-hand forms appear to develop slightly more power under experimental conditions but this is because the pad can be precisely ranged upon. An un-co-operative opponent would not provide the same opportunity!

Many senior martial artists consider the internal forms the most

This lock over-extends the elbow joint. Leverage is applied at the end of the arm

► Finger and thumb joints can be attacked by forcing the digit against its limits

►► The lock can be applied to two joints simultaneously. In this case, the wrist and elbow joints have been attacked

Throwing

1 Lean your body well forward and hook back with your right leg. Keep control over your opponent

2 Push him diagonally back over his trapped right leg and he will lose balance

efficient of the impact-based systems. This is one reason why, after a lifetime of training in external systems, they later change over. Actually, to develop power while relaxed is not at all easy and requires a great deal of training. It is often claimed that expertise in the external systems provides a good grounding for practising the internal forms.

LEVERAGE

Leverage makes use of simple physical principles to apply force out of all proportion to the effort used.

Consider the so-called Japanese arm-lever, where the opponent's elbow is hyper-extended across the forearm or shoulder by a pulling action. Leverage must be applied exactly on the joint – in this case the elbow – by pulling it over the shoulder, or by bracing it with the forearm, which acts as a fulcrum. Pressure must be applied as far from the fulcrum as possible. If this is done as described, a weaker person can overcome someone stronger. However, the lock will not work if the fulcrum moves away from the joint, or if leverage is applied too close to the fulcrum.

Leverage can also be applied against weaker joints. This is particularly useful where one of the partners is much weaker than the other. Not much pressure need be applied to the thumb or fingers to make an opponent submit. Finger joints can either be forced to bend too far, or they can be over-extended.

TRAINING AND TACTICS

Leverage force varies according to distance, so if you want to lock an opponent's shoulder you should apply force at his wrist. Joints such as the shoulder are heavily muscled and you may not be able to apply enough leverage against them. If this is so, go for weaker joints, such as those of the wrist and fingers.

The wrist is also a comparatively weak joint but the elbow and shoulder are progressively more difficult to lock. However, if leverage is applied to the full length of the arms, even the shoulder joint can be successfully attacked.

Leverage is also used to topple, or throw an opponent to the floor. The body is much taller than it is wide, making it susceptible to the effects of leverage, as can be seen in a simple backwards trip.

The attacker steps diagonally forward, so his right hip jars into the opponent's. As he steps, he swings his right forearm in a horizontal curving strike to the opponent's neck and leans well forward. He fetches his right leg up and insinuates it behind the opponent's. If the timing is correct, the forearm strike makes contact as the attacker hooks back with his right leg. Provided the

1

2

▼ *The forefist is perhaps the most used of the body's weapons. Conditioning is necessary to make it fully effective*

The 'wooden man' is a traditional Chinese training aid. The projecting spars teach how to attack through narrow gaps

opponent's head has been driven back and his right leg taken far enough forward, he will be levered diagonally backwards until he loses balance and topples onto his back.

TRAINING THE BODY'S NATURAL WEAPONS

The body's natural weapons are the parts which can be accelerated enough to develop impact force: the hands, feet, elbows and knees. The head also makes a formidable close-range weapon but it will not be considered here.

HANDS

Fist

Fore fist The most common hand weapon is the closed fist. Without proper conditioning, this is actually not the safest to use since your

knuckles are protected by only a thin layer of skin. To use your fists properly you need to toughen them. This procedure is not suitable for people under 18, because their bones aren't hard enough. Knuckle conditioning produces deformity and disfigurement even in adults.

The usual way to toughen your fists is with a punching post, a springy spar of wood firmly anchored to the floor. It is about 15cm wide and thin enough to bend on impact without breaking. Some punching pads are fixed against a wall but this is less effective and prolonged use can damage your wrist joints. The impact part of the pad is faced either with hard rubber or tightly bound with a rough string. Rubber damages the skin less and is more hygienic. A rough surface causes a thick skin callus to form, so protecting the underlying bones. This is better than damaging the bones so they respond by depositing extra material around injury sites because sometimes this bony callus interferes with finger movement.

The fist is driven repeatedly into the pad, so the fingers are forced back and the knuckles lead. Training starts gently and gradually builds over a period of time. Chinese systems condition their hand weapons with what is called the 'wooden man'. This is a vertical baulk of timber suspended between springy wooden bars. Short struts poke out of the baulk at different angles, representing arms and legs. The wooden man's body is used to condition the hands and the struts

DEVELOPING FORCE

▼ Hammer fist is used in a clubbing action. This technique requires less conditioning than forefist because the bones of the hands are well protected by muscle

Back fist uses the back of the knuckles to attack the face and head

toughen the forearms. Training is followed by treating the bruised hands and arms with a Chinese ointment.

Traditional Chinese conditioning methods also use canvas bags hung from the wall of the training hall. These are filled with dried beans, to which increasing measures of sand are added. The first pad is therefore quite soft and serves as the first stage of preparation. As training proceeds, the student graduates through increasing measures of sand.

Because of its rounded shape, not all the knuckles can be used in any punch, so different martial arts choose between them. Karate, tang soo do and taekwondo all use the index and middle knuckles. Kung fu schools generally use the lower three knuckles. Whichever the system, minimum preparation requires that the fingers are folded tightly, with the thumb lying on the outside, and a properly aligned wrist which doesn't bend on impact. Practice with an impact pad will develop correct application without

causing damage to the knuckles.

A prod with the end of a stick is painful because force is concentrated in a small area. This works with punches too and when the index finger is pushed out and locked with the thumb, it provides an effective weapon for striking the temple. The middle finger can be used as an alternative.

Hammer fist The closed fist is also used to deliver blows with the rolled little finger edge, usually in a clubbing action. The rolled fist pushes up a pad of muscle which protects the underlying bones, so it is safe to use against bony targets. It is always delivered with a circular action, the most common being an overhead strike that adds the weight of your descending arm to the impact. Last dynes of impact energy can be squeezed in by bending both knees slightly as contact is

about to be made. Hammer fist is also used for blocks, as described in the next chapter.

Back fist This uses an impact area on the back of your knuckles. Your elbow is raised until it points at the target, then it hinges so your forearm is driven out·in a circular strike to the side of your opponent's head. Your wrist is kept loose until the moment of impact and when your elbow suddenly stops straightening, your fist snaps out.

There are two different ways of delivering back fist strike. One uses a twisting action of your hips and upper body in the direction of the strike, whereas the other turns your shoulders away from the striking action, so your arm unrolls out. The first method seems to produce more impact but the second is faster and has greater range.

▼ *Knife hand is effective because it concentrates force over a narrow band*

Palm heel uses the pad of flesh at the base of the palm. It can be used with safety because the wrist cannot flex painfully on impact

Half-open fist This is useful for attacking through narrow openings such as below the chin and into the throat.

Palm heel When your hand is bent back it exposes a pad of flesh at the base of the palm called the palm heel. It makes an excellent weapon because the bones are well protected and the wrist joint cannot twist on impact. Chinese schools extend the fingers whereas in Japanese and Korean systems the fingers are half closed.

Chinese martial artists train for a strong grip by throwing a rough, heavy lump of rock into the air and snatching it as it falls. Okinawans use large stone-filled earthenware jars with necks sufficiently wide for the fingers to grip, lift and move the jars about. More stones are added as the grip becomes stronger.

Hand edge

Knife hand The edge of the hand below the little finger has become known as the karate chop, although it was used in jiu jitsu long before it ever became associated with Japanese karate. Knife hand is an effective weapon because it concentrates a lot of force over an extremely narrow band. The impact area is the pad of flesh which runs between the base of the little finger and the wrist. This is made more resistant to damage when the hand is slightly cupped and the fingers stiffened before impact. Knife hand serves equally well as a strike or as a

23

▼ Thai boxers use a downwards-travelling elbow strike to the crown of the head

▼ Spear hand is thrust
▼ deep into an unprotected part of the opponent's neck or body. This is a very dangerous technique

block. As a strike it is generally made with a circular swing, though it can also be used as a straight thrust to the collar bone.

Ridge hand Less commonly used is the hand-edge between the base of the index finger and wrist. This is used in a vertical circular strike to the opponent's groin, or as a horizontal strike to the throat or neck. The arm is swung in a circle, with the elbow bending slightly to correct for range.

Fingers

Many Chinese and Okinawan schools hone the fingers into fearsome weapons. The hand is extended with the middle finger withdrawn slightly to bring it into line with its neighbours. The hand is then thrust into the opponent in an action known as 'spear hand'.

Fingers are conditioned by driving them into buckets of beans, sand and stones. Sometimes bunches of bamboo slivers are tied together at top and bottom and the fingers thrust between them. When this can be done, the hands are thrust into stones heated over a fire! This is extremely disfiguring and results in loss of sensitivity.

◄ *Ridge hand is used in a swinging strike to the opponent's groin, or to his neck*

▼ *Knee attack can take several different forms. Most common is a vertically-rising strike*

▼ *A diagonal knee-strike works well against the solar plexus*

▼ *Thai boxers use a spectacular flying knee strike*

▼ *Thai boxers use their*
▼ *shins as striking weapons*

ARMS

Forearms

Not generally used for strikes, the forearm is effective for blocking.

Elbows

The elbow is a powerful and versatile short-range weapon. Typically your fist is clenched and the elbow swung upwards under your chin, horizontally into the jaw, vertically downwards onto the back of the lowered head, or straight back into your opponent's solar plexus. Slight shifts in weight increase impact.

LEGS

Knees

The knee is also an effective short-range weapon and is generally swung upwards into the groin/thigh, or brought diagonally around and into the solar plexus.

▼ *The edge of the foot is used in a variety of ways.*

1 In this case, it is thrust into the opponent's face

2 It can also be thrust into an opponent's ribs

Shins

Thai boxers use the front of the shin just above the ankle. As with the fist, this bony area is not well protected and some conditioning is essential. This is commonly produced over a long period by kicking bags of increasing density. Native Thai boxers hammer at their shins with bottles filled with sand!

▶ *The ball of the foot is a powerful weapon and can be used to attack both head and body*

FEET

Instep

The instep is similarly unprotected and suffers from injudicious use. The toes are curled downwards and the foot fully pointed until it is in line with the shin. Only when this flexibility is achieved can the weapon be effectively used. Impact is made just below the ankle; any lower and the foot is wrenched or the toes over-extended. A blow with the instep is delivered in an upwards snapping motion to the groin, diagonally to the thighs, or horizontally, to the ribs and head.

Toes

These are seldom used because they are so easily damaged, yet there are schools of Okinawan karate where they are toughened by kicking into pads. The big toe is effective because it concentrates a lot of force over a very small area.

Ball of foot

This is more generally suitable and can be used without extensive conditioning. However, the toes must be pulled up fully, or they will be forced back and injured and the instep needs to be in line with the shin to achieve good penetration. To develop position raise the heel high from the floor, while pressing down with the ball of the foot. Ball of foot kicks are delivered by

straightening the knee either vertically or horizontally. Vertical actions give rise to the front kick, horizontal delivery to the turning kick.

Sole of foot

This is used in Chinese and Korean systems in a thrusting action to drive an opponent back, or to check his advance. It is sometimes used against the knee joint.

Edge of foot

Below the little toe is known as the 'footsword'. The edge of the heel is also incorporated into a thrusting strike that drives the foot out sideways and into the opponent's instep, knee, hip, ribs or face.

Taekwondo athletes swing the vertical foot edge into the side of the opponent's head by means of a spectacular circling kick.

The inside edge of the foot is useful for scooping movements that strike and lift the opponent's weight-bearing foot. These techniques are used in jiu jitsu, judo and karate, where they are known as foot sweeps. Taekwondo and tang soo do athletes use the same part of the foot in a swinging strike to the face, or as an unusual block.

Heel

This may also be used in a thrusting strike to the groin of an opponent standing in front or behind. It is also

Axe kick uses a spectacular swing upwards, after which the heel is brought down on to the opponent's head or collar bones

used in that spectacular technique so beloved of karate, tang soo do and taekwondo, the axe kick, in which the foot is swung up until the knee slams against the shoulder; then it is dropped onto the opponent's head or collar bone.

USING AN OPPONENT'S OWN FORCE AGAINST HIM

If two martial artists take hold of each other and pit their strength directly, the stronger will win. If this were the principle of aikido, hapkido, jiu jitsu, judo and the grappling elements of shorinji kempo, there would be no point in weak people taking these arts up. However, early on in martial art development the principles of compliance and resilience were adopted.

You can resist if an opponent pushes hard and this will make him pile on more effort. If you then suddenly stop resisting and pull him, he will lose his balance and lurch forward. Conversely, if the opponent pulls hard and you first resist, then go with him, he will momentarily lose the initiative.

Compliance can be thought of in a slightly different way. If a brick is thrown at a plate of glass, the glass smashes. If it is thrown at a heavy curtain the fabric yields and absorbs the brick's energy, so it falls spent.

Putting these two concepts together, one can visualise an attacker lunging powerfully forward to seize an opponent, who steps back sharply and brings both hands up in a circular warding action. The attacker's arms are re-directed to

one side and his onrushing energy, finding no adequate resistance, causes him to fall forward. In another case, the attacker seizes the opponent's lapels and pushes him back. The opponent first resists the push and then suddenly pulls the attacker, falling back as he does. The attacker lurches forward and the opponent plants a foot in his stomach and cartwheels him over the top in an action known as the

stomach throw.

In the final example, the attacker throws a powerful straight punch and the opponent rolls with it, taking the wrist and drawing the arm out further. Instead of meeting resistance, the punch is pulled further out, taking the attacker off balance. The opponent's other arm locks the elbow and leverage is applied. The greater the attacker's force, the harder he will fall!

STANCES

Many classical martial art traditions lay great emphasis on stance — the way the feet and hands are positioned to produce a posture suitable for executing a technique. Indeed, traditional Chinese martial artists maintain that an exponent's ability can be immediately assessed by the quality of his stance and guard alone.

The training sequences known as patterns provide a good opportunity to practise stances in a flowing, changing way; stance should not be thought of as fixed or static. In the cut and thrust of an engagement, you must evade attack, close or open distances and be ready for all possible techniques by keeping your balance. All this comes down to mastery of stance.

Stances can be roughly classified into two broad divisions. The first is

▶ Patterns are excellent for improving stances. They also develop whole-body endurance, balance and speed

▼ Stand erect with shoulders relaxed and hands against the thighs for ritual stances

the ritual stance, and the second the practical stance. It is said that all martial art practice begins and ends with courtesy — hence the exchange of salutations before and after training. Martial arts can be abused, so there were many ways of testing a novice before he was admitted into the secrets of the tradition. Much of this testing is not done now but elements of ritual remain.

RITUAL STANCES

The ritual stance is one of attention and respect; attention to the teacher and respect for both him and your classmates. Usually it is erect, with heels together and the palms of your hands pressed flat against the front of your thighs. Your back is straight and shoulders relaxed with your head raised. There

Kneeling meditation
The back is upright and body weight settled on the backs of the calves. Practise maintaining this stance over increasing periods of time

Lower your body slowly to the floor. Hold the lowest position for a few seconds, then slowly return to an upright position once more

TRAINING AND TACTICS

Don't think of stances as rigid. They are fluid postures, functioning as platforms from which you initiate actions. It isn't enough simply to be able to take up a stance: you must practise moving between them. Only then will you be able to maintain the correct distance and line from a moving opponent and be poised and able to choose from the widest variety of responses.

are, of course, differences between the traditions but they all comply with this general description.

KNEELING MEDITATION

In some schools training is preceded, interrupted, or followed by periods of kneeling meditation. This is done by dropping to your haunches, with widely separated knees. First your right knee is pressed to the floor, then the left brought down to it. Finally your body is lowered onto the backs of your calves with your feet pointing straight out behind. Some traditions allow your ankles to flex, so the balls of your feet press to the floor, but others say this shows a poor awareness of danger. Someone stepping (inadvertently or otherwise) on the achilles tendons would injure the flexed ankles but not the extended feet.

Your back must be upright and your head held erect. Kneeling students of shorinji kempo are tested by pressing a staff to their backs and their stance is adjusted until their shoulders and the back of their heads touch it.

KNEELING STANCE

The kneeling stance is used for the ritual of respect which precedes karate classes. From this position your upper body is slowly inclined forward and your hands slide from your knees and press palm-downwards to the floor. The more martial-minded schools insist that you look forward during this but

◄ The Chinese martial
artist demonstrates
respect by enclosing
his fist with his hand
and bowing towards
his opponent

▼ This is a high stance
▼ from which fast
movements in any
direction can be
made

▼ A high stance allows
attacks to be made
quickly

PRACTICAL STANCES

READY STANCE

Once the appropriate opening ritual
has been completed, the class
moves to the next state of awareness. Typically this involves sliding
your feet a shoulder width apart
and clenching your hands into fists.

Your weight is evenly distributed
over both feet so you can move off
in any direction.

This is a practical and non-specific
stance from which others can be
generated.

WALKING STANCE

Either foot can take a half-pace
forward, your body weight shifting
to a mid-point between them. This
stance has length and width: the
half-pace between the heel of your
leading foot and the toes of your
rear foot are its length and the
shoulder width between the inside
edges of your feet give it width.

This stance is more stable than
the ready stance and can resist
pushes from the front and back, as
well as from either side. Your knees
are not bent, so it is a high stance,
allowing for rapid changes of distance or direction, making it popular in sparring. Sometimes your

less conscientious schools allow
your eyes to drop to the floor.

ERECT STANCE

Returning to the erect ritual stance,
some Chinese traditions begin training by stepping a half pace forward,
settling weight over your rear leg
and placing your fist against the
palm. Your upper body is then
turned through an arc. The way the
fist contacts your palm varies
according to the form of address
used. Shorinji kempo practitioners
raise both hands in front of their
face, pressing the palms together
with fingers splayed in the traditional Buddhist gassho.

Fighting stance is longer than walking stance but shorter than forward stance. It is a good compromise between stability and movement

▼ *This is an extremely long stance used during basic punching exercise. It is useful for strengthening the muscles which hold the knee joints together*

weight is transferred slightly forward and your rear heel allowed to lift. This, too, is a versatile stance, widely used in kendo.

FIGHTING STANCE

Your leading leg advances a further half step but maintains the same width. Your centre of gravity returns to a mid-point position and both feet turn parallel at a slight angle from straight ahead. Your knees bend equally, giving this new stance a measure of springiness.

This is a fighting stance, well suited to fast movement, but because it is longer it also provides good stability against an attacker's forward advance. The object is to present as small a target area as possible, which is why the body turns part sideways.

FORWARD STANCE

Your front foot advances a little further, so it is now a good pace and a half in front of the trailing one. Your hips turn square on and

Back stance is a polarised stance, with most of the body's weight over the rear leg

▼ Cat stance is adopted only fleetingly. Here the user has drawn back his front foot to make the kick fall short

BACK STANCE

Your centre of gravity is next brought back towards your rear leg by dragging your front foot back and slightly inwards. Both your knees are bent but the rear more than the front because of unequal weight distribution, your rear leg supporting 60 per cent of your weight.

This stance is normally used when an opponent withdraws slightly from the attacker's advance in preparation for a block or counter-attack. It has no width, so it is unstable to side attacks.

your shoulders are relaxed. Your rear leg acts as a prop and its knee straightens. Your weight shifts forward. Your rear foot should face diagonally forwards while your front foot points directly ahead. The length of this stance varies according to the martial art school.

The forward stance is used a great deal in basic punching and kicking exercises. It is also used during fast advances, combined with straight punches. However, because it is such a long stance the number of techniques which can be effectively applied from it is limited.

Longer stances lead to slow movements but they strengthen the muscles which locate the knee joint. This may seem incidental to the purpose of the stance, but the knees come in for a great deal of punishment and any method of helping them survive is to be encouraged.

Crane stance is adopted to lift the front foot clear of a footsweep, to perform a kick, or to begin an advance

Cat stance is polarised, with virtually all the body weight resting on the rear foot

CAT STANCE

Your centre of gravity is brought further back until 90 per cent of your weight rests over your rear foot. Your hips turn until they are facing forward and your front heel rises from the floor. Your rear leg is now well bent, so your height is the same as in the previous, back, stance. This posture has little width or length.

It is a polarised stance, from which the range of techniques are restricted. Usually it is transitional. As a stance in its own right it is useful for launching front foot kicks because the centre of gravity is so far back that the front leg can be used quickly and without telegraphing intent to the attacker.

CRANE STANCE

This is the ultimate polarised stance,

▶ For straddle stance sit down mid-way between your splayed thighs, keeping your back straight and your knees and feet pointing in the same direction

▼ The hourglass stance is a stable stance maintained by strong, whole-body muscle action. The heel of the leading foot is in line with the toes of the rear foot

in which all your weight is transferred to your bent back leg and your front foot lifted clear of the floor. Obviously this is unstable and is adopted only fleetingly before a more practical alternative.

STRADDLE OR HORSE STANCE

In this your feet are more than shoulder-width apart. Typically your knees are above your feet, rather than dropping inwards. Your back is straight and head erect, backside tucked in and hips raised. Sumo wrestlers turn their feet outwards, so they are parallel with the angle of their thighs. Other traditions keep the feet parallel, forcing the thighs outwards against the knees.

HOURGLASS STANCE

Horse stances are particularly favoured in the Chinese systems. They have width but no length and so are vulnerable from in front and behind. This can be remedied by reducing the width of the stance, and taking one foot forward so the heel is in line with the toes of your rear foot. Your feet are made to converge slightly and your knees forced either inwards or outwards, depending on the style. Your hips are raised and brought forward.

This peculiar stance is a favourite of many schools because it provides an excellent way to develop isometric muscle strength (the muscles contract but the joints they are attached to do not move) and is in any case a very strong and immovable posture.

TRAINING AND TACTICS

Stances are not only technique launching platforms, but also function as training aids. Low stances strengthen the muscles of your upper leg and this in turn benefits your knee joints. Postures such as 'hourglass stance' *work muscle groups against each other and build resistance to impact. High stances allow faster initial movements and low stances help you to 'dig in' under a strong attack. Some stances are general, others are highly specialised.*

LINE

Line is the positions taken up by two participants. Imagine that both adopt a left fighting stance as they face each other. In the first example A's leading foot is in line with B's rear leg, and vice versa. Both face each other square-on. From this position, both participants have an equal opportunity to use all their body weapons.

In the second example A steps slightly to the right, so his leading foot is now in line with B's. A then turns his body, so he faces B. Provided the sidestep is both un-obtrusive and not excessive, B may

◀ Scissors-step behind your front foot to launch a side kick

▼ Advance quickly by skimming your rear foot past the front of the supporting foot. Use this action to launch a front or a turning kick

supplying additional power for the following kick. Your rear leg is brought forward so it crosses the front one, the extent depending on the distance to be closed. Your front knee remains bent, so avoiding an energy-wasting bobbing motion. The kick is then performed as the step is still accelerating and in this way your forward body movement is harnessed to the kicking action.

Different kicks use different methods of stepping. For example in a one-step side thrust kick your rear leg steps behind your leading foot. In this way your hips are

not notice that it has been taken. What are the effects of this change of line? Simply that A can still use all his body weapons to attack B, who can only use his left arm and foot. If he wants to use his right side he must first twist slightly, which warns A. The concept of line is used extensively in points-scoring impact-based competition.

MOVEMENT BETWEEN STANCES

Stances are fluid and movement between them must be both smooth and fast. Normally this can be achieved with a simple step forward but some of the more polarised stances need specialised methods.

SCISSORS STEPPING

In a fast advance from a fighting stance to deliver a front kick the step is used as an accelerator,

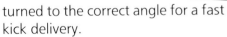

turned to the correct angle for a fast kick delivery.

Transition from horse stances also use the scissors step.

FLYING SCISSORS MOVEMENT

In more advanced techniques your rear leg skims forward in a low hop and even before your full weight descends on your heel your kicking leg is already lifting. This requires good co-ordination but greatly helps distance closing and impact.

SEMI-CIRCULAR STEPPING

The hourglass stance advances with a peculiar semi-circular step in which your rear foot curves inwards past your leading ankle and then sweeps back out to a new forward position. Your front foot first turns outwards to facilitate the step, then your rear foot moves as your centre of gravity shifts forward. Semi-circular stepping is also used from more general stances and it is usual-

37

▼ **Turning**
▼ **1** *Step across with your rear foot. Keep both knees bent. The distance which you step will determine the width of your final stance*

2 *Twist your hips, then allow your shoulders to follow. Turn strongly and be prepared to block*

Arrow walking
Use this movement both to cover distance and to change line

1 *Arrow walking begins by extending the front foot and then drawing up the rear foot. Take care not to shorten or elongate the stance*

2 *Extend your step forward from a fighting stance by . . .*

ly combined with a turning motion of your body to keep it aligned with your opponent.

ARROW WALKING

This is a method of making small advances and withdrawals by sliding your front foot forward and then drawing the rear one after it. Both parts of the step must be the same length, or your stances get successively longer or shorter. You can cover greater distances by sliding your front foot forward, then u-stepping into, and past it. This is very confusing and makes it difficult for your opponent to guess your intention.

TURNING

You can turn in a number of ways. The most common is simply to step across with your rear foot, which

must slide an equal distance from one side of your leading leg to the other. If not, the resulting stance will be too wide or too narrow. Both your knees should be bent and the

turning motion begins from your hips. Your shoulders momentarily lag behind, making use of a twisting moment in your spine to provide additional power. Then they swing

3 ...sliding forward on your leading leg

4 Draw up your rear foot...

5 ...and step out with your leading leg

▼ **1** Bring your front foot
▼ back, then slide it out to the side

2 Twist your hips around and be prepared to block strongly

around and you take up a new guard. You can turn through more than 180 degrees by stepping more widely with your rear foot.

Front foot turns give a fast, 90-degree change of direction. Your leading foot is drawn back to the rear one, then moved to the new position, your hips rotate and after a short delay, your shoulders follow.

The guard places your hands and feet in such a way that you can both defend yourself and counter-attack easily

GUARD

The guard is the position of your hands in relation to your stance. Some guards are defensive, protecting whole areas of your body and head from attack. Others are transitional and represent a short-lived fending off before counter-attack. Other guards are ritualistic and serve to warn your opponent off. However, all guards have certain general elements. Except in certain of the kung fu crane forms, one guard hand generally leads the other, providing an 'early warning' response, since it is further out from the body and so closer to the attacker. The kung fu dragon stylist uses his leading guard hand as a sensor, groping forward until it makes contact with the opponent, and following that contact with a rapid attack. However it is used, the leading hand lies in the projected centre-line of the body and the elbow is bent.

The rear guard hand is held closer to the body and on the centre-line. This provides a second barrier to an incoming attack and in long-hand boxing forms also makes for a strong punch.

If your left foot leads, for an effective defensive guard your left hand also leads. If you lead with your right your stance is opened up and your opponent given greater opportunity for attack. It therefore follows that the position of your guard must be related to your stance, the one changing as the other does.

TRAINING AND TACTICS

Carry your arms in such a way that you can use them either as deflectors of incoming attacks, or as weapons. The forward arm is closer to your opponent and so has the shorter distance to travel. It can also stop attacks early on, preventing them from building up too much energy. The rear arm provides a second line of defence and is 'cocked' ready to deliver a powerful strike.

BLOCKING

Blocking is used in all the martial arts to prevent an opponent's attack from succeeding, usually by interrupting and/or evading it. These are two quite separate techniques, though they occur together.

EVASIONS

Evasion is moving your body, or part of it, so the attack aimed at it misses. However, you must evade in the right direction: it makes no sense to move sideways and into a roundhouse kick, for instance. Similarly, it is not a good idea to run forward onto the attacker's straight punch. Therefore the first element in blocking is to work out what technique the attacker is about to use.

Having done that, the next stage is to make the evasive move at the correct time. If you move too early the attacker will note the change of position and alter the angle of attack to compensate. Conversely, leaving your evasion too late will permit the attack to strike home.

The third factor is to evade by the correct amount. Step too far and the attacker's fist misses by a long way and that's how far your counter-attack has to travel! You should move the minimum distance, so the attack misses, yet be left close enough to respond without delay.

You can evade an attack by stepping back, forward, to either side, or on the diagonals.

Backward A step back is the most

obvious, but its length is critical for your follow-up. You can either take a full step back, or simply step back with your rear leg and draw your front to it, shifting your centre of gravity over the rear leg.

Forward Curiously, a step forwards is sometimes a useful evasion, particularly when the attacker

is using a circular technique. It is unlikely that you will be able to take a full step forward, so a sliding action of your front foot will suffice. Thrust for this action is provided by bending your back leg.

Sideways You can take side steps by simply sliding out the chosen foot half a pace and drawing the

Draw back by the shortest distance necessary to make an attack miss

BLOCKING

1 *Thrust forward into an opponent's turning kick and counter-attack him*

2 *Step to the side with your front foot and twist your hips, so the attack passes across your front*

3 *Thrust forwards and to the side, so you both evade your partner's attack and close distance with him*

other leg to it. Your body turns slightly under the influence of hip action, so all your body weapons are available and pointing towards your attacker. You can also make side steps from long stances, where one foot leads the other.

Diagonally This posture also favours diagonal evasions which are useful for closing or opening distance. Your leading leg slides both forward and outwards, then your hips turn strongly so your body turns to bear on the attacker. Alternatively your rear leg slides diagonally back and your leading foot is drawn to it to prevent the attacker from stepping onto it as he advances.

Competition (especially ones involving several rounds) requires whole body endurance, flexibility and power. Mental motivation – the will to win – is no less a vital ingredient for the successful performer

BLOCKS

Blocks interpose a part of your body between the attacker's limb and its intended target. Usually the block is a limb, with your hand the most frequently used. Blocks are also used as weapons in those external martial arts which generate a great deal of force, but generally they provide insurance in case the evasion fails.

A classical allegory is helpful in understanding how blocks should work. A Chinese cook by the name of Ting was responsible for cutting up meat for banquets. The lord of the castle watched him at work and was amazed at the way his knife slid effortlessly through the carcass and with every cut, the meat fell from the bones. When questioned about his skill, Ting explained that some cooks need to sharpen their knives every week or so, whereas his was sharpened once a year. The reason was that he never cut through tendons, or hacked bone. Instead, his knife slid between the natural spaces within joints, and parallel to the tendons rather than through them.

The moral is that efficient blocks do not pit strength against strength unless it is the opponent's intention to do so. The best block is one which deflects the attack, not one which stops it dead in its tracks! This deflection involves meeting the technique along a line of weakness and exploiting that weakness.

The attacker may throw a straight punch, which you stop on the palms of your hands. This illustrates the

BLOCKING

Do not meet force with force. If you do, the iron bar will undoubtedly win! Try to redirect force by providing it with a sloping path

▼ *An x-block absorbs the energy of impact by allowing the arms to slide against each other. If the body then twists, the attack is thrown to the side*

► *Use the forearm in an upwards-rolling manner to deflect an attack. This is an effective short-range block*

attacker backwards. If he is standing on one leg executing a high kick, the push will dump him on his back.

A descending strike to the head with a pole is best dealt with by stepping forward to close distance and reduce force. Next raise a blocking arm sharply, with the underneath of the forearm forward, which protects the bones with a sheath of muscle. Point your blocking arm diagonally upwards and out from your body, so it meets the descending pole as low down as possible. Your forearm is angled, so

it forms a channel along which the pole slides. Provided your elbow is higher than your head, the pole will slide down your arm and drop harmlessly off your shoulder.

You can also use a double block, crossing your arms at the forearms, stepping in and catching the pole in the vee of your forearms. Your arms slide over each other so the pole's force is spent before it reaches your head and a sideways evasion then throws it away from your body.

Chinese systems use an elegant rolling and rising block that deflects

meeting of forces; the greater succeeds. If this same punch is struck to the side, it will miss the target. The incoming punch can also be knocked upwards, so it skims harmlessly over your head. However, to have the maximum effect, you must make contact as close to the attacker's wrist as possible, so you can use the principles of leverage, which may prove difficult against a fast moving punch.

The turning kick presents a quite different problem. In this case the attack path is curved so the block must get behind the foot and help it on its way. You must either draw back from the kick or move inside it by means of a sharp advance. At first this might not seem a wise move but circling kicks develop most of their power at the end of the leg and the closer in you get, the less blocking force you need. If all else fails, you can simply push your

▼ *Forearm blocks can be used in several ways*

The first (1) is like a windscreen wiper, intercepting the attacker's forearm with the thumb-side of the wrist

The second method (2) swings the little finger side of the wrist against the opponent's forearm

upwards a straight punch to the face. The horizontal blocking forearm rotates as it rises, increasing deflection energy. Attempts to poke at a spinning drum with a stick will show how the principle works.

Mid-section blocks generally use the forearms because they are fairly long and sweep a wide area clear, whereas hands are seldom longer than 22 centimetres, so blocks which use them must be very accurate. Basic forearm blocks use a windscreen wiper action, striking the attacker's forearm with the thumb-side of your wrist. Alternatively they use a clubbing action that swings your forearm into the side of the punch. Sometimes both arms move together in what is called an augmented block, in which additional energy comes

1

2

from your shoulder action.

Whether all this force is necessary depends on the particular martial art. One elegantly simple forearm block drives the open hand out from the waist and across the centre-line of the body. From there it curves outwards, hooking the incoming punch to the side with a fast movement.

Circular blocks sweep a very wide area and can be effective against all types of attack. Their principle can be illustrated by straightening both arms and then circling them in opposite directions across the front of your body and face. This allows the arms to first collect attacks, and then to sweep them to the side.

Palm blocks are very fast and can be used in a straight, thrusting action or as part of a circular evasion movement. They require good

▶ Step back and block an attacker's punch... ▼ *... then pull back the blocking arm and thrust out a reverse punch*

accuracy to be effective. Knife blocks use the little finger edge of the hand in a chopping, circular action.

The knees make effective if brutal blocks against turning or diagonal kicks. You simply rock back onto your rear leg, at the same time raising your leading knee and turning it into the kick. Taekwondo and tang soo do athletes use the inside and outside edges of the feet to bat an attack to the side. Foot sword can be driven down onto a

rising knee to prevent a kick from developing.

The way in which blocks are used is interesting because it reveals a number of fundamental differences in teaching method. Often a block is followed with an immediate counter-attack. The attacker lunges forward and punches to the opponent's head, the opponent steps back and deflects the punch upwards with a head block then slides forward on his front leg, withdraws the blocking arm and simultaneously punches. This is known as a serial sequence; one in which techniques follow on from each other. In practice the counter-punch must follow the block so quickly that the attacker has no time to withdraw his spent punch and launch another.

In the second case the attacker uses the same opening move but this time the opponent steps back

BLOCKING

▼ Make contact with the attacker's punch at an early stage

▼ Twist your hips and redirect his punch across the front of your body. At the same time, perform an uppercut to his jaw

▼ Step back and
▼ deflect the punch with a curving forearm block that continues in to strike your opponent's jaw

► Aikido techniques do not oppose force with force; rather they redirect the attacker's strength so it can be used against him

and twists his body sideways-on. The back of his leading hand contacts the incoming punch at an early stage and guides it harmlessly past the front of his face. Power for this action comes via hip rotation, and this same source is used simultaneously to thrust out an uppercut to the chin. In this instance the block and punch have been delivered at the same time.

The third instance begins with the same attack but this time the opponent steps diagonally back with his rear leg and crouches into horse stance, withdrawing his leading guard hand to power a circular counter-punch. The forearm is rotating as the punch curves home, knocking the attacker's arm upwards and continuing on into the side of his jaw. In this example the block is the counter-punch.

The second and third examples illustrate concurrent blocking and counter-attacking. Though this is both faster and more effective than block/punch sequences, it is also more difficult to teach in large classes, which require that complicated sequences be broken down into simple sub-units and taught by numbers. Unfortunately this must be unlearned later and the sequences re-integrated once more.

AIKIDO

The name aikido is composed of three Japanese characters, successively meaning harmony, energy, and way. *Ai* is linked to *ki* to imply a harmony of effort or force, meaning that the attacker's strength is harmonised with, rather than opposed. This concept is one which will be encountered again in jiu jitsu and judo. It is a yielding to the attacker's force but more than

that, it also means adding to that same force. In other words, it is an active form of compliance. The attacker pulls, the opponent does more than merely give way; he pushes, so his force is in harmony with the attacker's. This is a core principle of aikido.

The character *do* occurs frequently in Japanese and Korean martial arts. It indicates a path to follow, a route to understanding. The *do* is a

way of life, pervading all aspects of living and showing itself in attitude and manner. The follower of the *do* is always quiet, modest, and unassuming. These qualities derive from the martial art mind which has become cleansed of all passions and fears. The learner thinks 'Can I succeed? Will I lose?' The master acts instinctively with an uncluttered mind. He does not think, he acts.

The Way is a hard one and full of arduous training. The student receives little encouragement, for he must find the Way within himself — it cannot be imported from outside. The master merely nurtures and brings it on, often through acts which appear incomprehensible to the Western student.

Novices consider the technique of aikido as all-important, yet they are the easiest part of training. It is comparatively easy to become a consummate technician but incredibly difficult to defeat the self. Learning the techniques is only a vehicle for developing the Way. Defeating the self is the only way to mastery.

HISTORY

MORIHEI UESHIBA

Morihei Ueshiba (1883-1969) was such a master. He was the son of a farmer and from earliest days was strongly spiritual. Work on the farm builds strength and endurance, and early accounts of Ueshiba's life describe him as forceful and vigorous. He became interested in the Japanese martial arts and travelled

Tomiki aikido tests the effectiveness of its techniques in competition. Tanto randori *uses defence against a rubber knife*

to Tokyo, where he studied under Toszawa Tokusaburo of the *tenjin shinyo ryu* jiu jitsu school.

Conscription interrupted his formal studies and sent him to the Russo-Japanese front line. Ueshiba found other martial artists among the ranks of his unit and together they continued to practise informally. When he was demobilised Ueshiba was appointed a teacher in his *ryu*. He then joined a different tradition, this time taught by the illustrious Takeda Sokaku, who had been taught by Saigo Tanomo, himself descended from the Aizu warrior clan.

During the 250 or so years of the Tokugawa Shogunate armed warfare was stamped out and the warrior caste encouraged to turn its attention to more peaceable pursuits. This inevitably led to a decline in martial ability, especially in those clans which associated closely with the royal court. Outlying rural clans were not continuously subject to this debilitating influence and the Aizu were less affected than most. As a result their training system survived longer, under the name *oshikiuchi*.

Takeda studied *oshikiuchi* and modified it to suit current practical requirements. The result was an effective self-defence system which he named *daito ryu* jiu jitsu, in honour of General Yoshimitsu Shinra Saburo, the noted martial arts exponent who identified the key elements of distance and timing in martial art engagements.

Takeda was teaching self-defence to the Hokkaido police force when Ueshiba came in contact with him. Ueshiba avidly absorbed the traditions of *daito ryu* and in 1917 he was awarded a teaching diploma in the system. Then he had a mystical experience, which was to change the subsequent course of his life, in which he saw a vision of the unity of nature. This profoundly affected him and in 1938 he founded a new tradition based on natural harmony. The system was named aikido.

This founding of a new martial tradition through sudden enlightenment is by no means uncommon in Japanese history. It is said that many martial *ryu* were founded as a direct result of a flash of divine insight.

Aikido became popular and Ueshiba soon acquired a reputation as a powerful martial artist. It was only later in his career that he turned from physical force and wholly embraced the notions of harmony. Some of his students were not happy with this change in emphasis and broke away to found their own schools of aikido.

TOMIKI KENJI

Notable among these was Tomiki Kenji, who sought ways of testing the efficacy of aikido techniques through free sparring. This concept was anathema to Ueshiba, leaving Tomiki with the option of either giving up the notion of sparring, or leaving to found his own school. In the event he chose the latter and set up the Tomiki School of Aikido.

Interestingly, this development was paralleled in karate, where the Okinawan master Funakoshi tried to stop his senior student from studying free sparring, forcing him to leave and found his own tradition. This shows up a fundamental difference in attitude between those who taught martial art as a vehicle for improving self, and those who saw the practical value of its techniques. Whether a sporting vehicle is a sound one for testing real-life effectiveness is debatable because all combat sports must use rules and these, in turn, alter the character of the martial art itself.

The Tomiki School set up forms of competition in which techniques are tested against single attackers, two attackers working together, and single attackers wielding practice knives. Responses must be made according to the notions of good aikido technique and strategy.

Yoshinkan aikido uses strikes such as metsubushe *to divert an opponent before a hold is applied*

SHIODA GOZO

Shioda Gozo was another of Ueshiba's senior students who, through a disagreement over the effectiveness of aikido technique left to found his own school, the Yoshinkan. Though both Yoshinkan and Tomiki School are interested in testing aikido techniques, the Yoshinkan disapproves of competition and relies instead on non-point scoring free sparring engagements. Shioda left Ueshiba fairly early in the latter's development of aikido, so his aikido reflects an intermediate stage in the tradition's development. Accordingly there are links with jiu jitsu in the form of locks which work against the joints. It also features diversionary strikes which attack the opponent's weak points before a hold or throw is applied. A typical example of one of these strikes is the *metsubushe*, a fist strike using the back of the large knuckles to attack the bridge of the opponent's nose, or his eyes.

KOHEI TOICHI

The cultivation of health through development of the *ki* principle of aikido was taken up by another of Uehsiba's senior students, Kohei Toichi. Kohei is deeply immersed in the generation of natural energy and uses his aikido as a vehicle for this. Some of the demonstrations given by his school are impressive and not easy to explain in simple physical terms. Classical aikido continues under the direction of Ueshiba's son, Ueshiba Kishomaru.

PRINCIPLES OF PRACTICE

Classical aikido does not initiate attack. The attacker must open the engagement for it is through his force that the harmony of aikido is brought into play. Whatever the attack, the *aikidoka*'s response must be one of harmony, so if the attacker steps forward and punches, the *aikidoka* will draw back. At the same time he will take hold of the attacker and pull him forwards. The attacker's own force is augmented, so he loses the initiative and is brought under control.

Aikido techniques are circular rather than straight-line. The attacker's impetus is never brought up short but rather deflected and steered by an applied curving force.

If an attacker stands off and snaps out fast punches, all but true experts will find it difficult to deal with him in the classical manner. An

▼ The classic aikido hold bends the joint in its natural direction

▼ **Falling**
▼ Spring forward on to the palms of your hands

▼ Roll forwards along
▼ the curve of your
▼ spine, lowering your head by tucking your chin to your chest

aikidoka tries to use distance in such a way as to make the attacker over-extend. Tomiki competition requires him to rush forward with his arm extended in an obliging manner. Demonstrations of classical aikido also rely on the attacker

lunging forward. Non-classical, practical *aikidoka* advise using a pre-emptive strike to distract the partner, then quickly applying a hold and/or throw.

The classic aikido hold applies leverage to the wrist, forcing it to bend further in than it ordinarily would. This is more efficient than forcing the wrist back because the muscles concerned are weaker. The elbow too is locked by aikido techniques but this time by using leverage against the joint's natural action. The shoulder joint is over-extended by means of an arm lever.

TECHNIQUES

Falling

The first thing the novice *aikidoka* learns is how to fall safely by converting the energy of falling into a rotating movement. Roll-outs are learned through a form of progression, so the student can feel how the body moves, and later extend this to more complicated developments.

You begin from a squatting position, extending both arms forward. Then you drop your hands to the floor, toppling and rolling forward with head tucked in and spine curved. The energy of forward movement rolls you over until your hips contact the mat, at which point you gather your feet together and stand up quickly.

When you are quite confident you next roll-out from a standing position, leaning forward and touching the floor with your right

hand. You simply roll forward along the line of your arm, and then down across the shoulders to your hips. Once you can do this, the next stage is to jump forward and roll-out.

Some aikido schools practise forward roll-out by jumping high over an obstacle, hitting the floor and immediately rolling. This is good fun provided the students can roll-out easily from the static position and the floor is well matted.

Back roll-outs are first learned from a squatting position. You unbalance yourself backwards, falling onto your backside and rolling up the curve of the spine to your shoulders. Next you try it from a semi-squatting position and so on, until you can roll-out from standing upright. Sometimes an excess of momentum will roll you backwards and over your head. If this happens you arrest the movement by bringing your feet in and together, then standing smoothly, in one movement.

Elbow lock

In the first example of aikido technique you step to the left, avoiding your attacker's rush forward. You seize his outstretched right arm in your left hand with an over-hand grip and then both pull and draw him around, never letting him regain the initiative. Rotate your body, hooking your elbow over the top of your opponent's right arm and pinioning it against his chest with the little finger side turned upwards. Then brace your left arm by bringing the right across and under it, which

▼ **Elbow lock**
1 *Seize the attacker's outstretched arm and draw him forward, so he loses his balance*

2 *Lift his wrist while bearing down on his extended elbow. Keep his arm close to your body*

▼ **Wrist twist**
▼ **1** *Seize the attacker's wrist with both hands and bend it back towards him. At the same time, step smartly around with your rear foot*

2 *This action applies a painful torsion to your opponent's wrist and forearm, throwing him on to his back*

1

2

prevents your attacker from freeing or twisting his arm out of the lock. If the technique has been applied properly, it will conclude with the attacker on his knees, his right arm fully extended and twisted, and held tight against your chest.

wrist, bending it further in the direction that its fingers are pointing. This causes excruciating pain and brings the attacker to his knees. Your circling movement then topples the attacker down onto his right side. The attacker's right elbow must be bent for the wrist lock to work well and you must keep your elbows in as you step.

Wrist turn

The final sequence uses a circular lock application to the wrist from a stationary position. The attacker seizes your right wrist with his right hand, using an overhand grip. You move slightly towards the attacker, so his right arm is forced to bend slightly at the elbow, at the same time bringing your left hand down on the back of the attacker's hand and turning his right hand in a circling movement. The little finger edge of your right hand curls over the attacker's wrist as your left hand keeps his hand trapped. The lock is applied by rotating the attacker's forearm.

Wrist twist

The next sequence starts with the same attack but this time you seize and bend the attacker's right wrist. At the same time step quickly around and apply pressure to his

1

2

BUDO AND BUJUTSU

When battlefield experience was examined, it was seen to provide a core of knowledge useful to other members of a particular school and as time passed, this core of knowledge was added to until it became a martial tradition, or *ryu*, teaching military arts, or *bujutsu*. The leaders of the Japanese warrior caste began systematising their training from the late 12th century onwards, and by the 17th century, an incredible 9,000 *bujutsu ryu* existed!

What were the classical military techniques? *Bujutsu* was based on the effective use of a small armoury of weapons, the principal one being the warrior's sword. Swords were the warrior's badge, the emblem of his caste and all that he stood for. Skill in wielding the drawn sword

was only one requirement, for the warrior also needed to draw and use the sword quickly in one fluid action. This dictated a number of appropriate postures and stances, all of which were taught within a number of *bujutsu ryu*.

The bow and arrow was a favoured weapon, used both from horseback and by infantry formations. Spears tended to be used by rank and file combatants, though some warriors of noble birth trained with them as a speciality weapon. Halberd training featured in many *ryu*, because this weapon proved to be extremely effective at dealing with mounted warriors. When horses became scarce, the halberd was relegated to the role of specialist weapon. It was also introduced as a home defence weapon for the wives of warriors.

Hardwood staffs and short sticks were not considered noble weapons though their effectiveness was well known, and many warriors trained with them if only to discover their weaknesses. The iron-staff was bound with strips of iron and though forming a part of *bujutsu*, it was so physically demanding that its use was not formally taught within the *ryu*. Several other weapons were taught in *bujutsu ryu* but they were all speciality weapons and were not widely used by classical warriors.

Sometimes combatants closed to the point where they could grapple. The classical warrior fought in armour, so apart from knocking an opponent over with a particularly powerful blow or kick, striking

techniques were not particularly effective. Warriors grappled to allow a dagger-thrust, or to restrain a captive while he was being bound.

The mounted warrior was obliged to handle his horse effectively, guiding it by knee pressure alone as he aimed his bow and arrow. More than 50 *bujutsu ryu* taught methods of achieving skill in horsemanship. Swimming too was elevated to the rank of martial art and warriors were taught how to swim strongly in armour, how to grapple while in water and even how to use weapons while afloat or partly submerged.

The Edo period of Japanese history extended from 1603 to 1868 and was a time of relative peace under the Tokugawa military rulers, during which martial arts development effectively halted. Tremendous changes had occurred in *bujutsu*. The introduction of firearms had radically altered the way battles were fought for even when wielded by a master, the sword was no match for muskets in the hands of conscript soldiery.

To divert an idle warrior caste from creating strife and yet maintain a reserve of martial ardour to use in the event of a foreign invasion the Tokugawa *bakufu* encouraged splintering within the feudal estates, so the ruling lords (*daimyo*) found it difficult to put together durable power blocs. At the same time, the military ardour of potential conscripts from the non-military castes was increased by allowing their participation in what came to be called martial ways, or *budo*.

◀ *The halberd was used as a home-defence weapon by samurai women*

▼ *The halberd can be thought of as a sword blade attached to a long handle. Halberds used for competition sometimes have a wooden blade*

The martial way differed from the martial art in that battle-effectiveness was no longer the over-riding consideration, so other factors could be taken into account. The need to defeat the self became the new prime objective. This, of course, was also a requirement of *bujutsu*, so a change of emphasis rather than a change of concept provided the foundation for *budo* and made it acceptable to the warrior caste. In any case, the declining ability of the warrior caste, weakened as it was by the absence of warfare, meant undiscerning acceptance of changes to technique. Freed from the necessity for effectiveness, martial techniques developed according to other priorities.

FULL CONTACT

The impact-based martial arts are karate, tae-kwondo, tang soo do, kung fu and Thai boxing. Each has its own system of competition which varies from non-contact through to full contact, in which blows of uncontrolled force are delivered.

It is worth considering the effects of full power blows to the head. The brain is composed of soft tissue enclosed within a bony skull and every time the head is struck, brain tissue is jarred. Every time the head is jarred backwards, inertia jams the brain tissue against the bones of the skull. The results of this is to kill off thousands of brain cells. When someone gets a bang on the nose blood flows and the damage is obvious. When brain cells are destroyed, there is no obvious injury, though the victim may complain later of headaches and inability to concentrate. Providing the damage isn't too serious and the brain tissue is allowed to heal, brain function is unlikely to be badly impaired. If, however, the brain is repeatedly damaged the effects drastically multiply until in chronic cases the martial artist becomes punch drunk. So many brain cells have been killed off that brain function is irreversibly damaged.

SEMI-CONTACT

In recognition of this some systems use what is called semi-contact. One form allows full contact to the body but no hand contact with the face or head. Full power kicks to the head are permitted but these are so infrequent that the risk of brain damage is minimised. However, kicks are very powerful and even single impacts can cause serious

Full-power kicks and punches to the head may cause no obvious damage but they destroy brain tissue

damage. This form of semi-contact does not allow padding on the feet, though headguards are allowed in certain schools.

The second form of semi-contact allows blows to the head and face, though they must be controlled and any blow which causes injury is penalised. Padding on hands and feet are used to reduce impact. The final type of competition involves no contact whatsoever. This is extremely difficult to judge and nowadays it has largely fallen into disuse.

DEVELOPMENT

Full contact was devised as a way of allowing all the impact-based martial arts to compete and at first, matches between kung fu and karate, or taekwondo were quite common. Later, when the tactics of fighting to these rules became better developed, martial art distinctions vanished and full contact became a fighting art in its own right.

TRAINING AND TACTICS

You must withdraw from sparring for six weeks if you are momentarily stunned by a hard blow to the head. There may be no blood or obvious damage but your brain will have suffered injury and must be allowed to recover fully.

TECHNIQUES

As its name implies, full contact uses punches and kicks of unmitigated force against the head and face, with the object of knocking the opponent out. Participants wear light plastic boots over the instep and ankle, leaving the sole exposed, and normal boxing gloves.

Many people enjoy full-contact training though, perhaps not surprisingly, few actually enter the ring to compete. Training is arduous but highly practical, with the emphasis on the high-level endurance that allows a fighter to maintain power throughout a multi-round match. At first, classical martial artists wrongly imagined that they would need no more than one round to defeat an opponent but with blows padded by gloves and boots, this proved not to be the case.

Classical techniques tended not to work in the full contact ring. Particularly disappointing were the turning kicks — so devastating in the classical training hall, yet ineffective in the ring. This was primarily because the classical stylists trained for perfection of form, repeating their kicks against the air. When these same kicks were delivered to an unfriendly martial artist, they lacked impact. Punching bags inevitably modified technique and second-generation turning kicks could not be used against the empty air — they needed impact with a resistance to maintain balance.

Punching bags are usually filled

◀ Some types of semi-contact use padding on the hands and feet

▼ Classical striking techniques sometimes gave disappointing results in the full-contact ring. This resulted in revised training methods which used punchbags and impact pads

Target mitts or small impact pads are ideal for accuracy training

pace drops down to a tickover, to allow fatigue poisons to be pumped out of the muscle. After a minute or so, tempo increases once more to full output. The cycle is repeated several times, after which a full leg-stretching programme begins. A partner is used to hold the bag and prevent it from swinging wildly.

Punch bags are also invaluable for developing full power strikes. You begin by delivering single jolting impacts into the bag, then punch in flurries of blows. Your body leans in behind each blow, your chin tucks in and your punching shoulder leads. Circular punches are used a great deal because they are difficult to avoid and clip the side of the jaw, causing it to rotate sharply and produce a knock-out.

Target mitts are of little use for developing power but they are excellent for improving timing, accuracy and speed. The target mitt is a fingered glove, the face of which is covered by a firm pad. Your partner holds the pad at the correct height and angle where you can hit it by a selected technique. The mitt faces square-on for jabs, sideways for turning kicks and angled for hooks.

Reaction timing is improved by suddenly holding up the mitt and turning it so you must decide the best weapon to use on it.

When you are reasonably competent at this, two mitts are used, one held low and the other high. They are moved in a slow weaving pattern, inviting flurries of different techniques. Your partner moves forward and back, to one side, then the other, until after long hours of practice, you can hit a moving target with a high degree of accuracy. Full contact uses most of the arsenal of striking techniques, except those which cannot be adapted to gloves and boots.

After a short time students are ready to spar with each other, but only controlled blows are allowed. Headguards and shinguards reduce the possibility of injury still further until all that is left is an exhilarating but still violent combat sport. Only those with a killer instinct need consider going into the ring!

In many ways full contact is similar to Thai boxing and to *la savate* (French boxing). However, unlike Thai boxing, it does not allow elbow and knee strikes.

with rags, until they weigh about the same as the average man. They must be soft enough not to damage the legs even after repeated impacts, yet heavy enough to provide resistance. You begin by kicking the bag lightly, performing perhaps five kicks on one leg before changing over. The pace of training gradually increases until the blows are going in at full power. Still later, you kick the bag at full pelt for a full two minutes, after which the training

HAPKIDO

The name hapkido consists of three Korean characters which mean way of harmony. Hapkido regards itself nowadays as a practical form of self-defence, a vehicle for maintaining the practice of old Korean martial traditions, and a combat sport.

HISTORY

It might appear at first that Hapkido is no more than a Korean school of aikido – especially since there is no record of hapkido in Korea before the Japanese invasion in 1909. Hapkido techniques have some

similarities to aikido but use more locks which work against the joints. It also uses classic jiu jitsu body drops and throwing techniques which indicate that if hapkido is indeed an offshoot of aikido, it is from an early version.

This view is complicated by the uniquely northern Chinese/Korean high circling kicks which have no place in aikido and until the 1960s, no place in karate either. Breaking techniques are also practised and this, again, is another uniquely Korean characteristic. Hapkido involves weapons work, using sword, staff, short sticks and butterfly knives but curiously there is no record of spear forms, though they may have been present in the original tradition. Striking techniques and weapons forms appear, however, to be relatively late additions, rather than core features. Interestingly, there are hapkido schools which have none of these additions and these closely resemble an original aiki jiu jitsu ancestor.

The obvious conclusion is that hapkido derives from both modern and ancient, indigenous and foreign systems. When trying to identify the elements which contributed to present-day hapkido, it is necessary to look for stylistic similarities rather than functional ones. There are only a limited number of ways to attack the wrist, so many different systems have arrived at the same applications of leverage without being connected, but non-functional similarities in what otherwise seem to be distinct arts are evidence of a common origin.

Hapkido and aikido use similar mannerisms, particularly in the way the index finger points during grip application. This habit was developed from Japanese aiki jiu jitsu, the forerunner of aikido, where it was believed to channel the flow of living energy known to both Japanese and Koreans as *ki*. Even though the index finger is not generally used in the classical gripping action of many traditions, it is rare to extend it. A second but less significant similarity is in the usage of the roll-out to dissipate landing force after being thrown.

During the setting up of the Korean Taekwondo Association, hapkido was pressured to join with other schools into one umbrella body. The principals declined to do so and affiliated themselves instead to the Department of Education.

TECHNIQUES

The principles of hapkido are taught at three levels. The basic level

◄◄ *Hapkido uses locks which work against the joint. This technique over-extends the elbow joint and is the basis for a throwing technique*

◄ *Hapkido grasps use an extended first finger*

▼ *Hapkido attacks nerve points to produce a disproportionate reaction to the degree of force used*

Here the defender is simultaneously attacking his opponent's left hand while

preparing to strike his right with a one-knuckle punch

Throwing

1 *An opponent seizes both your wrists*

2 *Step across and break his grip by circling your hands against his thumbs*

3 *Take his left arm and lever it against his right elbow*

4 *Use this leverage to throw him*

teaches straight kicks and punches, the intermediate level evasions and re-directions and the advanced level teaches circular techniques. Straight techniques are used to initiate an attack, evasion techniques can be used offensively or defensively, and circular techniques are used defensively. The attacker's strong moves are responded to with soft techniques that deflect them from their target and bring them under control, while not pitting strength against strength. A weak attack is replied to with a strong counter. In both cases, the object is to gain control of the attacker quickly.

STRIKES

Strikes are made in two ways, the first a sledgehammer blow that bruises or damages and the second a precise application of force to one of the 300 nerve points used by hapkido masters. Koreans inherited elements of Chinese medicine which believes that the body con-

tains invisible channels along which energy flows on its way to invigorate bodily functions. These channels come near the surface and/or cross at various points and it is here that the application of force is most effective. However, it is claimed that energy flows along these different channels according to some kind of diurnal timetable, so there is little

point in striking at one, unless energy is actually flowing through it. If this is done, then the flow of energy is stopped and distal parts of the body suffer in consequence.

THROWS

Hapkido throws are spectacular in their effectiveness and elegance.

1

2

3

4

Throwing

1 *Step across and break your opponent's grip. Grasp his wrists*

2 *Turn your back to him and lever his arms down on your shoulders*

3 *Throw him over your back*

1

2

3

The following example uses the opponent's arm to lever him into a cartwheel, dumping him helpless on the floor. It is used when an attacker seizes your wrists in preparation either to kick you in the groin, or pull you off balance. As soon as the grip is applied, step across with your front leg and turn your body until it is three-quarters on. At the same time circle your hands, moving them against the weakest elements in the attacker's grip — the thumbs. Grasp your attacker's left wrist with your left hand and his right wrist with your right hand. Then rotate your hips strongly, using this energy to

Leg trap
1 *Block your opponent's kick with an x-block*

2 *Seize his ankle and twist it, then swing your right leg over the top*

3 *Force him face-down to the floor and twist his ankle*

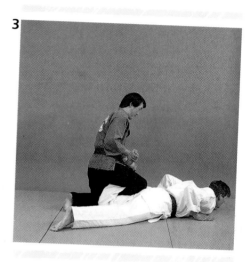

bring the attacker's right arm underneath your left elbow and lever his forearm against your own right elbow. This applies a painful twisting action to the shoulders and cartwheels the attacker onto his back. You maintain grip during the throw, so the attacker remains under control.

A very similar movement uses the same opening sequence. The double wrist grab is broken by circling the trapped hands against the attacker's thumbs. You seize the attacker's wrists, then step across in front of your leading leg, at the same time forcing the attacker's left arm under your right. Extend both arms as you use hip action to turn under them. Bring the attacker's elbows down against your shoulder, which acts as a fulcrum. Pressure on the captured wrists then hurls the attacker over your back and onto the floor.

A particularly interesting technique in the hapkido syllabus is a leg-trap that counters the attacker's kick. Your attacker takes up a left stance, you adopt a right posture. When range has been set up correctly, the attacker uses a front kick to your mid-section. You slide back your front leg, transferring weight above the left, at the same time using an x-block and grasping the attacker's heel. The attacker is drawn forward and his leg trapped by a double-handed grasp. You swing your left leg in an inside-circling kick which curves over the attacker's trapped leg and jams down behind his knee, forcing him to the floor and into a leg lock.

COMPETITIONS

Competitions are similar to karate matches, with one referee, four judges and an arbitrator. A scale of points is awarded according to the quality and technical difficulty of the technique used, and an immobilisation lock or choke hold earns a technical knockout. When scores are equal, the refereeing panel decide on the relative merits of the two performances. Matches last for three minutes of actual fighting time but during the finals there are two three-minute rounds, with a rest of one minute between them.

There are also competitions involving patterns, weapons work, self-defence and breaking boards. In each case, a panel of five adjudicators score each performance to a 10-point maximum. The form competition is interesting in that it awards merit points for a correct variation in the relative speed of successive sequences. This is rather unusual for Korean patterns, where all moves tend to be made at the same speed.

Weapons forms use short sticks, staff, quarterstaff, longsword(s) and butterfly knives. Sometimes two longswords are used in a manner vaguely like Chinese *wu shu* performances. The self-defence competition takes the form of pre-arranged performances which demonstrate responses to set attacks.

IAI JUTSU
AND IAIDO

ai jutsu is the Japanese martial art of drawing a sword. Sometimes the name *batto jutsu* is used, though this implies striking with the sword immediately it is drawn. Techniques for drawing and using the sword were taught in more than 400 martial *ryu*, the earliest being found in the *tenshin shoden katori shinto ryu*.

HISTORY

Many *ryu* died out during Japan's peaceful Edo period, as the military importance of the sword declined in the face of firearms. Opportunities for sword-drawing in a practical way diminished, so elements of ritual began to enter into practice. One of the earliest was the way some schools of iai jutsu restricted sword-drawing techniques to those made from a formal kneeling position. Not only was this an invalid stance for effecting a quick draw, but seated action was only one part of a much wider field. Some schools restricted teaching still further and ignored the short sword altogether. Hand in hand with this dilution of training went an increase in participation as uncritical non-military personnel were admitted into membership of the newer *ryu*.

The purpose of training changed so that effectiveness in drawing the sword and striking down the opponent came to be replaced by the cultivation of a calm, martial arts mind, in which no thoughts of self intrude to upset the operation of non-discursive action.

Iai jutsu is the martial art of drawing and striking with the sword

▶ *The cut is made with a drawing action that enhances its effect* ▼ *The cut has been made, the sword is re-sheathed, but concentration remains*

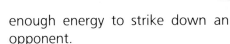

TECHNIQUES

The elements of iai jutsu can be summarised into four actions, the first being the draw, or *nukitsuke*. This must take into account the starting posture, the relative positions of the hands and blade, and the speed at which the blade is withdrawn from the scabbard. Normally it should be accelerating throughout this movement so that when it is unsheathed, it already has

enough energy to strike down an opponent.

The second element is *kiritsuke*, the cutting action. The sword is either plunged into the opponent, or it cuts him, using a drawing action of the blade. An effective cutting action demands proper technique and this was learned by slicing through bamboo poles or straw bags in a drill known as *tameshigiri*. A row of poles were set in the earth at intervals and the swordsman practised a series of fast, flowing cuts against them. A poor action knocked the poles from the ground, or failed to cut them cleanly.

The third element of iai jutsu is *chiburi*, or removing blood from the blade. This is achieved by wiping it with a piece of paper or cloth. Blood has an extremely corrosive effect on the steel blade, which must be thoroughly cleaned soon after use.

▼ The iaido draw is made from a kneeling position

▶ The cut is made in one fluid action

Finally the sword must be resheathed in the action known as *noto*. This was a slow and deliberate movement, during which time the warrior remained in a state of great concentration, or *zanshin*. Iai jutsu training used the long and the short swords, since both were worn by classical warriors, and though the longer blade might have to be left behind on occasion, the short sword was always retained.

Various opening postures for fast sword drawing were considered and the two most used were a standing position and a semi-kneeling position which both left the long sword clear for a fast draw, and which allowed a fast shift of body weight. The two swords, or *daisho*, were carried on the left side with their cutting edges uppermost. This convention meant that the fastest cuts were made in a 'sky to earth fashion'. This contrasts with earlier sword-drawing techniques using a long sword known as the *tachi*, which was slung from the left hip and carried with the cutting edge downwards, necessitating a more effective (for the mounted warrior, that is) 'earth to sky draw'.

IAI DO

Metaphysical aspects of training, although an essential part of iai jutsu, became paramount in iai do, the way of sword-drawing. The term iai do only came into common use during the 20th century, though the principles which distinguish it from the original and effective iai jutsu go back more than 300 years. Modern iai do is greatly changed from its military ancestor, with virtually all effectiveness sacrificed to ritual flourishes. The sword is drawn too slowly for it to be immediately deployed and while it is being unsheathed, the swordsman is vulnerable. Because the modern exponent does not practise *tameshigiri*, he has little notion of how to make a cutting action. As a gesture towards cleaning the blade, the exponent now merely shakes it. Finally, the action of *noto* is now so quick as to serve no purpose other than a flamboyant demonstration of skill.

FIGHTING ARTS
OF INDIA AND PAKISTAN

Little has been written about the fighting arts of India and Pakistan though the ancient classics of Indian literature provide ample reference to them.

HISTORY

Hindu society depended on a noble warrior caste, the *kshatriyas*, to provide military support for a liege lord, or local king. This elitist caste developed traditions of fighting over a period of years. In the absence of wars military games maintained these traditions. Thus it was that the games, called *samajya*, came to include elephant combat, *must-yuddha* (muki boxing, which is still practised today), staff fighting and wrestling.

In a country as vast as India, many different forms of martial art inevitably developed and even in the vestiges left to the present day, some differences can be seen. Northern styles tend to use high jumps, expansive movements and kicks. Southern styles favour smaller movements and higher stances, using more arm than leg work. This pattern is repeated in China.

UNARMED COMBAT

WRESTLING

Indian wrestling pre-dates military tradition and has been variously known as *mallak-rida*, *malla-yuddha*, and *niyuddha-kride*. These names covered four activities, one of which was *dharanipata*, the tech-

niques of taking an opponent to the ground. It is not clear whether *dharanipata* involved striking techniques. *Asura* was a second type of wrestling and certainly did include striking. However, all blows had to be delivered above the chest if they were not to foul. *Nara* was a third type but no clear details about the rules under which it was fought have survived. *Yuddha* was an extremely bloodthirsty variant in which opponents frequently died from their injuries.

A further variant of Indian wrestling introduced during the Muslim conquests of the 13th century lasted until the arrival of the British in the 18th century when it declined and all but vanished. It owed its survival to the patronage of local princes in such states as Baroda, Indore, Mysore and Patiala.

Indian wrestling survives today in much the same form as it has been practised over the last 150 years. It is quite popular and in Lahore there are no fewer than 600 gymnasia today. Training begins early, with some students as young as six — though the average age for entrance is in the teens.

BOXING

Indian boxing is as old as wrestling and, as in the Greek pankration, contests were often lethal affairs. The advent of Western boxing in the 1890s eclipsed traditional forms with the exception of muki boxing. This extremely rough and violent activity can still be found in such places as Benares.

The system known as *marma-adi* uses pressure and strikes to vulnerable areas of the body. It is based on the theories of periodic energy flow through the body along certain lines called meridians. A blow on an active meridian is said to cause damage out of all proportion to the physical force used. *Marma-adi* teachings are taught secretly to selected students.

Striking techniques use all the customary hand and foot weapons, including the fore-knuckles, the hand-edge, the palm-heel, the fingertips and the elbow. Kicks are delivered with the ball of the foot, the instep, the heel and the big toe. Northern styles generally kick high, whereas southern schools seldom kick above the waist. Forms use sequences of techniques performed against imaginary opponents. They are analogous to Japanese kata and Korean poomse.

The village martial artist often also practises medicine — as in China. This is not as strange as it first might seem because in learning how to attack the body, it is helpful to know how it works.

ARMED COMBAT

SWORD

The typical Indian sword is less than a metre/40 inches long. It is light, well balanced and flexible, and was either wielded in pairs, or singly with a shield. Training drills use a recurring sequence of cuts and counters from opponents circling each other. No grappling is permitted. Training with the sword has now virtually died out completely. The spring-sword uses two or three sharpened bands of steel ribbon and is flailed in a circular manner. This had a strong deterrent effect but unless It caught the throat, it tended to inflict nasty gashes rather than fatal cuts.

SPEAR

The Indian spear is about 1.5 metres/5 feet long with a cord of equal length attached to the butt. This cord was wound around the thrower's wrist and allowed him to recover the weapon when it missed. The Indian spear was a cavalry weapon.

STAFF AND STICK

The Indian quarterstaff (*lathi*) is a near 2 metre/6-foot length of bamboo. It is bound with leather and weighs about a kilo/2 pounds. Quarterstaff training uses pre-arranged drills with a partner, free sparring taking place only when students are proficient. Competitions are held according to rules. Stick-fighting is also popular and lengths vary. Staffs and longer sticks are wielded with both hands whereas shorter sticks are grasped with one hand.

DAGGER

The dagger is a concealable weapon with many uses and a tradition devoted to its use grew up in Northern India, where the Bundi dagger was developed. This has a grooved double edged blade with a curious grip equipped with long metal wrist guards.

Competitions are held to assess the effectiveness of practice. These use pre-arranged sparring, though highly dangerous unprogrammed sparring occasionally takes place. An interesting variant pits an unarmed man against an opponent with a dagger. The unarmed opponent must disarm the adversary, secure the dagger and use it against him.

Weapons are normally used to injure, or to threaten injury. Except in police arrests, they are used less frequently to restrain an opponent physically. The techniques of *bandesh* were devised several hundred years ago to permit an armed warrior to use his weapon to immobilise the opponent by means of a joint lock or strangle.

Leverage moves the centre of gravity until it is no longer possible to compensate. When the point of no return is reached, the person falls or is thrown to the floor. Simple as that!

JUDO
AND JIU JITSU

HISTORY

Present-day judo and jiu jitsu come from many lines of development, some of which spring from the distant, feudal past of Japan. The earliest reference to unarmed combat is found in the eighth-century *Nihon shoki* chronicles. Interestingly, this same reference is also used to validate the sumo tradition and so it seems possible that sumo and jiu jitsu had common origins, though they have diverged widely since.

The first reference to jiu jitsu's direct ancestors does not appear until the 15th century. At that time the martial art tradition of *katori shinto ryu* developed a system of grappling to supplement its syllabus

of armed techniques. This became known as *yawarra ge* (the pacifier) but is not connected with the similarly named *yawara gi* of the *muso jikiden ryu*. The *tsutomi hozan ryu* developed its grappling system at the same time, calling it *yoroi kumiuchi* (grappling in armour). This was used when opponents closed inside sword distance, and it became necessary to grapple while reaching for a knife. Armour had spaces through which a heavy dagger known as the *yoroi doshi* could be thrust.

Partially or lightly armoured warriors used the system known as *kogusoku* which was developed by the *takenouchi ryu* and subsequently came to be known as *tori te*.

Sometime later the *yagyu shinkage ryu* improved both earlier forms and originated its own system, which worked equally well on armoured and unarmed personnel, called *araki ryu torite-kogusoku*.

Few of these early grappling arts were unarmed. Apart from *yoroi kumiuchi* using a heavy dagger, *kakushi jutsu* used concealed weapons, as did the 17th century *tai jutsu* (body techniques) of Kemmotsu Nagao. Oguri Niemon developed *wa jutsu* (techniques of harmony) for civilians and the first use of the name jiu jitsu (techniques of compliance) appeared in the late 17th century, though the art it referred to was more commonly known as *yawarra*.

Terada Kanemon taught the unarmed element of the military tradition known as *kito ryu* under the name judo, or 'way of compliance'. Continuing this development of unarmed systems, Iso Mataemon developed the tradition of *tenjin shinyo ryu* in the 19th century.

A sporting aspect is not new to jiu jitsu: during the 17th century wrestling competitions came to be very popular. It was principally by this means that jiu jitsu was first introduced to the non-military. Jiu jitsu's very popularity contributed to its undoing because as more people practised, so the mystique was lost. Furthermore, the various non-classical schools came into conflict with each other and violence was commonplace. Eventually the name of jiu jitsu was synonymous with violent behaviour and it fell into disrepute.

Present-day Olympic judo is descended from the ancient Japanese martial art of jiu jitsu

Jigoro Kano incorporated free sparring into his jiu jutsu and from this came sport-judo

JIGORO KANO

Jigoro Kano was born in 1860 and began to study the martial arts from the age of 17. He first joined the *tenjin shinyo ryu* school and learned striking techniques from Fukuda Hachinosuke. When he died Kano moved to *kito ryu* and studied grappling and throwing techniques with Ikubo Tsunetoshi. Kano also studied two classical *bujutsu ryu* and from all these synthesised *kodokan judo* in 1882. The prefix distinguished his art from the other forms of judo practised at that time. He intended that his art should be used to inculcate a healthy mental and physical discipline, suitable for being taught in schools. By choosing the right teachers and training them carefully, Kano's judo removed itself from its damaging association with the jiu jitsu of that era.

MARTIAL ARTS THEN AND NOW

The main function of martial arts – such as jiu jitsu – was to survive an encounter on the field of battle. By way of comparison, martial art ways – such as judo – are practised as combat sports, or as a means of disciplining the mind. Consequently the do forms have eliminated a great many effective techniques and replaced them with more ritualistic forms. The rules of competition favour particular types of strategy, so these have advanced at the expense off the older ways. The martial art changes to suit the purposes of practice.

Kano had incorporated a form of free sparring (*randori*) into his judo practice and this proved extremely popular. Judo's sporting potential emerged and in 1909 Kano affiliated it to the International Olympic Committee. For the next 29 years he served as Japan's representative, dying in 1938 on his way back from promoting judo overseas.

The opponent's own momentum is a powerful ally, to be used against him. All throws must begin with a movement that creates momentum, which then powers the throw

Jiu jitsu principles of leverage are used in judo throws and holds

Jiu jitsu techniques like this rear strangle are excluded from the judo sporting syllabus

DOCTOR YOSHITOKI

One of the foundations of judo and jiu jitsu practice is 'compliance' – yielding to the opponent so as to gain an advantage. The most commonly attributed originator of this principle is Doctor Yoshitoki, who is said to have been otherwise dismayed at the strength needed for the Chinese wrestling techniques he had studied. It is said that one day he was inspired by the way a willow tree survived a storm by bending before the wind and then whipping back unharmed afterwards whereas the more rigid cherry tree next to it was battered to pieces.

GENERAL YOSHIMITSU

Two further fundamental aspects of practice were identified by General Yoshimitsu in the school of aiki jiu jitsu. He studied the possibilities open to an unarmed warrior facing an opponent with a sword and concluded that mastery of distance was a key element. Timing was also vital, so the defender harmonised totally with the attacker, moving unerringly and unhesitatingly as he did.

Aiki jiu jitsu went into a decline after Yoshimitsu's death though it continued to be practised within his immediate family. However, during the latter part of the 19th century there was an upsurge of interest in the internal energy of the body – *ki* – and aiki jiu jitsu returned to popularity.

CHIN GEM-PIN

Jiu jitsu includes its own striking techniques for attacking vulnerable parts of the opponent's body (*atemi*). It has been suggested that the Chinese boxing master Chin Gempin is a source of these techniques.

PRESENT-DAY PRACTICE

Jiu jitsu practised in the present day can be divided into three main

◄ *No. 346 fails to apply leg reap because he hasn't barred across the opponent's chest with his left arm. The throw has therefore degenerated into a battle of strength against strength*

▼ *The thrower has dropped well below the hapless opponent's centre of gravity and timing, co-ordination, leverage and power combine to produce an effective throw*

▼ *Side breakfall is one*
▼ *of the most common ways of falling safely. It must be mastered before you can move on to practise throws*

Front breakfall uses spring in the elbow joints to absorb the force of landing

categories: traditional jiu jitsu based on the classical *bujutsu ryu*; non-traditional jiu jitsu originated in Japan, such as the *hakko ryu*; non-traditional jiu jitsu originated outside Japan.

Judo in the United Kingdom is regulated by the British Judo Association, which selects teams of *judoka* to take part in international competitions.

The British Judo Association operates a scale of adult kyu gradings:

9th kyu   yellow belt
8th kyu   orange blt
7th kyu   orange belt
6th kyu   green belt
5th kyu   green belt
4th kyu   blue belt
3rd kyu   blue belt
2nd kyu   brown belt
1st kyu   brown belt

TECHNIQUES

As you might expect, judo and jiu jitsu techniques are very similar to each other. However, judo has eliminated some of the more dangerous techniques.

Falls

Both judo and jiu jitsu teach how to fall safely and the method adopted is identical in both systems. Practise

a rear breakfall by sitting down on your haunches and then rolling backwards. Curve your spine and tuck your head in, so the energy of motion rolls you backwards. Bring both arms forward and then smack them back into the mat to arrest the breakfall. When you can do this easily, start from a semi-crouching position and eventually from a full standing position. Always tuck your chin into your chest.

Practise side breakfall by lying out on your left side. Then twist your body to the right and slap the mat hard with your extended right hand. Twist back to your left side and slap the mat with your left hand. Roll back and forth in this manner. Then practise from a crouching position by unbalancing sideways and falling into the mat. Finally stand up straight, swing your leg across the front to unbalance your posture and fall sideways onto the mat. Strike the mat hard, as before.

Front breakfall is practised from a crouching position. Fall forward onto your chest and strike down with both hands with your elbows bent. Fall forward from a standing position, taking the descending weight on both elbows.

Judo engagement begins with both participants taking a firm grip of each other's tunic, or judogi

Throw your head and shoulders into the throw, otherwise your opponent may succeed in turning the tables

Engagement

Engagement begins when the two *judoka* take hold of each other. *Jiu jitsuka* sometimes begin with one partner seizing the other, but generally the grip is made on the body, or on a limb, rather than on the training tunic. *Jiu jitsuka* also begin many techniques from a postures apart position.

Throws

Hip throw In a jiu jitsu throw from a postures apart position, your opponent throws a punch which you block with your left forearm. Continue the block into a circular *atemi* strike, using a palm-heel to the side of his jaw, but make the blow a glancing one; the object is to distract and not necessarily to knock out. The strike continues past the jaw and loops back around his neck. Step up smartly with your rear foot and swivel your hips around so you turn parallel to him. Step past his leading leg and bring your feet together. Loop your right arm around his back and take him forward and across your right hip.

Major outer reap Next try a basic judo throw from engagement position. Grasp your partner's right sleeve in your left hand, and his left collar in your right, step back slightly and pull him towards you, which

will make him rear back. Use this resistance to step alongside his right foot. Throw your head and chest forward as you hook back with your right leg into the calf of his right leg. If you synchronise the movement correctly, you will have taken his centre of gravity diagonally backwards and sweeping his leg will then topple him onto the mat. Don't step too far past him as you apply the throw, because it will take too long to reap back with your right leg. Also, don't wait too long

1

2

3

Throwing
1 *Block your opponent's punch with a forearm block*

2 *Lunge forward off your back leg and strike your opponent a glancing blow to the chin*

3 *Twist your hips and seize his right arm while encircling his back with your right*

4 *Drop below his centre of gravity and lever him over your hip*

5 *Dump him on to his back*

after you've pulled him forward and do throw your head forward – otherwise the tables may be turned on you!

Shoulder/neck lock

The second jiu jitsu technique uses a twisting defection to avoid a punch. Step across with your back leg and guard with the palm of your hand, then swivel your hips back towards your opponent, using this action to power a swinging forearm strike to the side of his neck. Transfer your weight forward to lend force to it. Keep your blocking hand on the attacker's arm. Your striking right arm curves around the side of your opponent's neck and you seize the wrist with your left hand. This locks his shoulder and neck as you take him to the floor. Maintain the hold, sinking your weight and splaying your legs widely to preserve balance.

TRAINING AND TACTICS

An opening diversionary strike creates an opportunity to attack, but beware! An opponent will not stand still as you try to throw him, so be prepared to apply the technique quickly and smoothly. If things don't work as you planned, go for an alternative throw but if you lack the skill, withdraw and wait for another opportunity. Don't wrestle ineffectually with each other.

4

5

Shoulder/neck lock

1 *Step smartly to the side and deflect your opponent's punch*

2 *Strike him across the throat with your right forearm. This technique is powered by hip action*

3 *Link your hands together, trapping his extended arm and applying a stranglehold*

4 *Lower your body weight and take him to the floor. Maintain the stranglehold but be prepared to release pressure the moment he taps you, or the mat*

▼ Body drop
Jump around so your back is turned to your opponent. Maintain your grip on his jacket and use hip action to draw him forward, over your hip

Use your hip to lever him up and over, so he lands flat on his back

1

2

3

Body drop

The final judo technique is a body drop. This is performed from an engagement position, your left hand gripping your opponent's right sleeve and your right arm grasping his left collar. Push him back slightly and then jump around, so your back presents to him. At the same time, sink down below his centre of gravity, so he does not have to be lifted up. Pull hard on his right arm, wheeling him around, so he overbalances across your right hip. Maintain control of him as he falls.

4

KARATE

HISTORY

Karate began on the island of Okinawa, then an independent nation, about 450 kilometres south-east of the Japanese mainland and 550 kilometres from China. Because of its geographical position, it was culturally influenced by both China and Japan.

Okinawan masters covertly visited the Chinese mainland to increase their martial art knowlege. Eventually three broad types of Okinawan martial art sprang up, named after the nearest city. Thus *shuri te* (hand of Shuri) was practised in and around the capital city, *naha te* was practised at the port of that name and *tomari te* flourished in Tomari.

Development continued and *shuri te* gave rise to what is called *shorin ryu*. This is a fast-moving style, favouring agile movements and skilful evasions. *Naha te* evidently followed closely on the classical Southern Shaolin kung fu systems for it was by turns both soft and hard in its applications, using higher stances, semi-circular steps and powerful circular strikes. It became known as *shorei ryu*. Both *shorin-* and *shorei ryu* were influenced by *tomari te*.

Okinawan masters organised a council, the Okinawan Shobukai. They chose the name karate (China hand) as an umbrella name for their various fighting arts. This title was adopted in recognition of the major role played by the Chinese in its development. The Shobukai selected the Okinawan school teacher Funakoshi Gichin to represent them publicly.

FUNAKOSHI GICHIN – THE FATHER OF MODERN KARATE

Funakoshi Gichin was born in Shuri, the capital of Okinawa in 1868. He was not a strong child so his family sent him to learn karate under masters Azato and Itosu. He became a competent, well regarded student and continued practising after taking up teaching.

In 1902 he demonstrated karate to Shintaro Ozawa, the commissioner of Okinawan schools, which led to the inclusion of karate in the schools' curriculum in 1903. In 1906 Funakoshi gave the first open demonstration.

In 1912 Funakoshi was chosen by the Okinawan Shobukai to give a karate demonstration to the Japanese navy and when this proved successful, he went on to give a series of demonstrations throughout Okinawa. One before the admiral of the Japanese Imperial Fleet stimulated interest in the mainland and in 1917 he visited Japan to give a demonstration at

Karate is an Okinawan martial art containing many different and diverse schools. Some schools use light, fast movements, others concentrate on great strength

Success requires indomitable spirit. There are those who enter the contest area as losers. Their ambition is to lose with as little ridicule as possible. This is not the martial spirit!

the *Butokuden*, or Hall of Ancient Martial Virtue. Later he returned to Okinawa and gave up teaching to promote karate full time. The Shobukai subsequently chose him to demonstrate karate to the Japanese Crown Prince.

In 1936 Funakoshi took on the mantle of leader of the Japanese karate movement. He changed the meaning of karate's name from China hand to empty hand and though pronunciation remained the same, a different Japanese character was selected to represent it. He also altered the titles of the old kata from Chinese to Japanese and although these actions were considered sacrilegious by some, obvious links with China were inappropriate at that time.

During that same year Funakoshi's students succeeded in raising enough money to build the first karate *dojo*. This was called the Shotokan, or Shoto's club, Shoto being Funakoshi's pen-name. He also published his second book on karate, *Karate-do Kyohan* or *The Master Text*.

During the Second World War there was a massive influx of students, but most of the most senior students were killed and the Shotokan was itself destroyed during an air-raid in 1945.

In 1947 Funakoshi began to rebuild karate. Curiously, although judo and the other martial arts had been forbidden by the occupying forces, the Americans didn't understand karate and allowed it to flourish unhindered. In 1949 Funakoshi was appointed chief instructor to the Nippon Karatedo Renmei (Japan Karate Association).

Funakoshi died at the age of 89, on 25 April 1957, leaving behind a legacy of practice and behaviour which survives to the present day as an example for all who would follow in karate *do*. The school he founded flourishes to this day and is the largest karate style in the world, with an estimated 10 million practitioners in 90 countries.

OTHER OKINAWAN MASTERS

Although Funakoshi is popularly regarded as the founder of modern karate, he was not the only Okinawan master to visit Japan and set up schools there.

Chojun Miyagi

He was born on 24 April 1888 in the Okinawan port of Naha. From the age of 14 he trained in *naha te* under the great master Kannryo Higaonna. When the latter died in 1915 Miyagi travelled to the Chinese mainland and studied the soft forms of kung fu. He combined hard and soft elements of practice and founded *goju ryu*.

His fame spread and in 1928 he accepted a teaching post at Teikoku University in Kyoto. This was only one of several temporary appointments and after a stay of a few months he returned to Okinawa. Miyagi continued to train throughout his life, visiting the Chinese mainland again in 1936. He died in 1953 at the age of 65 but the school he founded still flourishes.

Preparing for the finishing technique after successfully countering a roundhouse kick

KARATE THEN AND NOW

Karate developed in Okinawa under Chinese and indigenous influences. It was first known as Ryu kyu kempo ('Chinese boxing') and later as Karatedo ('Way of the empty hand'). It is an impact-based fighting system which is most effective at the middle distances of engagement. It generally relies on strong muscular action to develop force and so it is described as 'hard'. A competitive aspect has developed, with subsequent modification of technique. Karate is now recognised by the International Olympic Committee as a potential Game. There are four major schools of karate.

Kenwa Mabuni

He decided to cast his net as wide as possible and in addition to training with Miyagi's master, Kannryo Higaonna, he also trained under one of Funakoshi's teachers, Master Anko Itosu, and with Master Aragaku of *tomari te*. He also visited China with Chojun Miyagi and there studied southern *shaolin*. He eventually blended these different schools together in the style which became known as shito ryu.

STYLES OF KARATE

Okinawan karate was taught in a bewildering array of schools and this diversity carried over to Japan. The governing body in Japan is the Japanese Karate Federation, which has designated what it regards as the four major schools.

SHOTOKAN

This is the first all-Japanese school of karate. It was founded by Funakoshi Gichin who, in turn, drew on the knowledge he had learnt from masters Azato and Itosu. Shotokan is radically different from both its Okinawan predecessors. Its stances became lower and longer, with far greater emphasis on power generation by muscle spasm. Virtually all Shotokan's movements are performed in straight lines by moving either forward or backwards.

WADO RYU

This 'school of peace' is a Japanese

Knockdown karate allows full-power kicks to the head

school of karate founded by the classical martial artist, Hironori Ohtsuka. The style relies strongly on correct distancing and evasion, so the opponent's power is re-directed. Ohtsuka's skill in jiu jitsu resulted in a small number of wrist locks and throws being incorporated within the syllabus. Such techniques are rare in karate.

GOJU RYU

Chojun Miyagi's style is a mixture of hard external and soft internal systems of kung fu with indigenous Okinawan influences. It works well from close range and uses the *sanchin*, or hourglass stance for developing strength and stability. The body is extensively conditioned, using Okinawan training aids.

SHITO RYU

This karate syllabus contains the largest number of katas of any karate school. This is because Mabuni studied other styles and incorporated their kata into his system. Its stances are of medium height, with neither shotokan's length nor wado ryu's height. Its techniques are executed concisely, using short sophisticated movements rather than large, circular or straight-line ones. Although Okinawan in origin, shito ryu actively involves itself in competition.

SHOTOKAI

This school of karate is not regarded by the Japanese governing body as

one of the major styles, yet its history is interesting. It began by helping to found the shotokan but broke away in 1956 in a dispute over increasing commercialism and competition. The shotokai represents an early stage in the development of shotokan karate and differences between the two schools are striking.

KYOKUSHINKAI

Masutatsu Oyama's style means 'the way of ultimate truth'. Oyama has veered away from philosophising influences and regards his system as a practical form of fighting. The core requirement of the school is toughness and this is nowhere

The standing bow is an expression of respect for teacher and classmates. Make a standing bow even when there is no-one in the dojo

▶ *The grading syllabus introduces techniques according to difficulty. The early grades teach proficiency in the basic moves. Higher grades teach how to use these basic moves proficiently*

more eloquently seen than in kyokushinkai knock-down competition, where full power blows to the body and uncontrolled kicks to the head are allowed.

PRINCIPLES OF PRACTICE

Karate is practised in the *dojo*, or 'place of training in the way'. The traditional *dojo* is simple and scrupulously clean. The floor is of highly polished wood, though sometimes straw *tatami* or mats are used.

Courtesy

Remember to bow each time you enter or leave the *dojo*. Always perform the bow correctly – don't just nod briefly. Pause at the entrance, stand with heels together and hands against your thighs. If a higher grade is already inside, bow

to him. If there is no-one in the *dojo*, bow towards the centre, or towards any object of honour, such as a wall scroll, or photograph of the school's founder. Bow slightly and hesitate when your head reaches the lowest point. Don't bow so low that you can't keep your eyes on the high grade. Once you have made your bow, step out of your sandals and walk onto the training area.

Behave correctly in the *dojo*. Speak only when you are spoken to by the coach, or by senior grades. Don't lark about, laugh, or otherwise misbehave. Always sit down with your legs crossed so no-one will trip over your feet.

The lesson begins when a higher grade calls the class to order. Form lines according to your grade and stand with heels together and feet splayed. On the command *'seiza!'*, drop smoothly down on your right knee. Keep your back straight and your arms by your sides. Lower your left knee and sit back with your head erect, back straight and palms down on your thighs. On the command *'sensei ni rei!'*, slide your hands to the ground in front of your knees and lean forward. Keep your eyes on the coach. Maintain the bow for a second, then straighten up. The coach will return the bow. Repeat the kneeling bow, this time to your classmates. The command for this is *'Otogaini rei!'* On the command *'kiritsu!'*, rise to a standing position with the reverse action to that used during kneeling.

If you arrive late and the class has already started, don't just enter the

dojo and join in. Perform a standing bow in the doorway, then drop into *seiza*. Make two kneeling bows and remain kneeling until called in by the coach. If you need to leave the *dojo* during the course of training, first ask the coach for permission. If he is busy, ask a high grade instead.

GRADING SYSTEM

Your progress through karate is measured by means of the grading system. This divides up the school syllabus into six, eight, or nine parts called the *kyu* grades. Each grade is identified with a coloured belt.

Originally only three coloured belts were used – white, green and brown but other colours have been added and the following is a typical sequence:

Novice	*red or white belt*
8th kyu	*white belt*
7th kyu	*yellow belt*
6th kyu	*orange belt*
5th kyu	*green belt*
4th kyu	*purple belt*
3rd kyu	*brown belt*
2nd kyu	*brown belt*
1st kyu	*brown belt*
1st dan	*black belt 1st level*

You take a practical examination at each stage. The average time between gradings is a three-month period, or 48 hours in all, whichever is the greater, but between 2nd/1st kyu and 1st kyu/1st dan it is six months or 96 hours.

The average student achieves black belt in about five years. You

have mastered the basic techniques of karate when you reach this stage. However, black belt is not an end in itself because it too, contains stages known as the dan grades.

Dan-grade examinations may be taken according to the following timetable:

2nd dan	1st dan must be held for 2 years
3rd dan	2nd dan must be held for 3 years
4th dan	3rd dan must be held for 4 years
5th dan	4th dan must be held for 5 years
6th dan	5th dan must be held for 6 years
7th dan	6th dan must be held for 7 years
8th dan	7th dan must be held for 8 years
9th dan	8th dan must be held for 9 years
10th dan	9th dan must be held for 10 years

Only the founder of a school may hold 10th dan, though some founders consider that they are beyond grade. Ninth and 10th dans sometimes wear red belts, signifying that they have travelled a circular path of

knowledge and returned to a symbolic beginning of training. Seventh and eighth dans can wear a belt with alternating red and white bands. The body of black belts within a school is called the *yudansha*.

Gradings are normally carried out by the club coach. Usually he can assess students to within two or three grades below his own level, so first dans may grade up to third *kyu* brown belt and third dans to first dan. Students carry a licence book recording their current grading.

After the ritual courtesies warm-up exercises begin. These warm your muscles, making them more fluid and able to stretch quickly and without injury.

Basic techniques

Warm-up is followed by the basic techniques of karate: individual punches, kicks, strikes, or blocks, performed to the coach's count. The class advances up the *dojo* in lines and at the end the coach calls out '*mawatte!*' and the class turns in unison. As they turn, they make a loud shout, the *kiai*.

Kiai comes from the action of the diaphragm muscle, not from higher in the chest. When you push a heavy object such as a car, you may grunt with the effort. This is the same source as for *kiai*, which is deliberately made loud to demonstrate your fighting spirit and the strength of your technique.

Combination techniques

The next part of the syllabus to practise is combination technique, or *renraku-waza*: combining basic moves in a logical sequence, one leading naturally into the next. Many combinations of basic technique are possible and skilled students select their own. Combination technique produces the ability to deliver a whole series of techniques, rather than a single one which may be blocked.

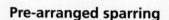

Kiai *is a shout made with the diaphragm. Use it to extract the maximum power from your technique*

▼ *Kata teaches rhythm, balance and concentration*

speeds and in different directions. Each kata may take many lessons to learn but after much practice, you forget technique and your mind is free to concentrate on its deeper meaning. At this point art transcends technique and the way towards true mastery of karate becomes illuminated.

Kata

Kata builds endurance of precisely the right type to benefit karate practice. It also teaches technique, rhythm, balance and concentration. Kata always begins and ends on the same spot. The content of some kata can be explained by means of a training method known as *kata bunkai* (analysis).

The beginner finds kata difficult to learn, for it initially appears to be no more than a confusing sequence of techniques performed at varying

Pre-arranged sparring

Pre-arranged sparring between pairs of *karateka* is known as *yaku-soku kumite*. The attacker is referred to as *tori* and the defender as *uke*. Pre-arranged sparring allows students to practise the principles of

◄ *Agility, skill, speed and stamina are improved by kata*

▼ *Pre-arranged sparring teaches distance, timing and control*

requires that though the attack is pre-selected and performed in a realistic manner, the response to it is unplanned.

Free sparring

Jiu kumite should only be practised by those grades capable of forming the correct body weapons and of controlling the force used. In this form of practice both attack and

TRAINING AND TACTICS

Free sparring requires a great amount of skill and control, so don't begin sparring until you know how to form body weapons correctly and have practised against an impact pad or punch bag. It is always best to delay free sparring practice for as long as possible. I would suggest until at least green belt.

distance and timing safely in ·response to an attack in a way that is not possible with kata training. The attacker is restricted to using a single specified attack and the defender must respond with a specific counter. In three-step sparring, the attacker makes three successive attacks, each of which is systematically countered. The last counter is followed by a counter-attack that ends the sequence. Five-step sparring uses the same principle with five attacks.

At first the attack/response sequences are simple but as the pair become more experienced, they become more complex. Although attack and defence are always agreed beforehand, they are each performed more naturally from a fighting stance. *Jiu ippon kumite*

KARATE

Most injuries occur during free sparring. It is essential that you have a reasonable standard of skill before attempting it

defence are unplanned, though dangerous techniques – such as open-hand attacks to the eyes – are prohibited. The school may allow quite substantial body contact between partners of equal weight, but strikes to the face and head are always strictly controlled. Sometimes the force of attacks is reduced by mutual agreement to touch contact.

TECHNIQUES

These techniques are the foundation on which technical excellence is built, the individual units of practice which the expert assembles together to produce a flowing attack, or an effective defence and counter.

1

2

Lunge punch
1 *Begin from forward stance with your leading arm in the lower guard position*

2 *Step forward with your rear foot, keeping your arm extended and both knees bent so as to maintain a constant height*

3 *Step into the new position, still with your arm fully extended*

4 *Thrust your arm out strongly as you withdraw the other*

Lunge punch (*oizuki* or *junzuki*)

This relies on the moving body to generate impact power and to re-duce recoil. The punch is delivered with the same leading leg and fist so if the left foot leads, the left fist also leads.

Begin practice from forward stance, or step back from ready stance with your right foot while sweeping your left arm down and across the body in left lower guard position (*gedan barai*). Begin by skimming your right foot forward a full pace. Your left knee remains bent; straightening it will create a bobbing motion. Leave your left arm out during the step, and don't move it about.

Move your body weight forward behind the advancing foot and as it settles, pull your left arm strongly back to your left hip. Use this action to help thrust out your right fist, both arms travelling at the same speed. When your punching arm is at full reach, the forearm rotates and the knuckles turn upwards. This is paralleled by the left first, which twists knuckles-downward.

Your upper body leans slightly into the punch, your elbow locks and your left knee straightens fully, all at precisely the same time, the point of impact, with the whole body committed to delivering maximum force. Immediately after-wards, all muscles relax, ready for the next move. Punches to the head are called *jodan*, to the mid-section *chudan* and to the lower stomach and groin *gedan*.

Reverse punch (*gyakuzuki*)

This is one of the most used karate techniques. Unlike in lunge punch, the opposite fist and leading leg are extended, so greater hip movement is needed to get effective range. Some schools step directly from one reverse punch stance to the next. Others use a semi-circular step.

Begin from left forward stance, with the left arm extended down-

3

4

▼ **Reverse punch**
1 Begin from forward stance with your arm extended

2 Wind your hip back and then twist it forward again, using this action to thrust out a strong reverse punch

3 Drive your body behind the punch, withdrawing the other fist to your hip

4 Some schools step forward in a semi-circular manner with the rear leg. Others simply step directly forward. Whichever method is used, maintain a constant height

5 Place your foot in the new forward position but leave your arms as they are

6 Punch strongly as weight descends on the new front foot

wards into a lower guard position. Wind back your right hip, then twist it forward. Your shoulders do not immediately follow but first allow tension to build in the spinal muscles. This is then released and

the punching shoulder swings forward. Allow your rear foot to swivel with the hip movement, so it comes to point more or less directly ahead. Use pull-back of the left arm to power the punch and just before

impact is made, both forearms rotate in unison. Your stance is now set up to begin advancing reverse punch practice.

Begin by stepping forward with your right leg. Make the step either

▼ **Front kick**
▼ **1** *Begin from fighting stance, or forward stance*

2 *Raise your knee to the correct height and pull back your toes*

3 *Thrust your foot out into the target, extending your knee joint fully to achieve maximum range*

4

5

6

3

Front kick (*maegeri*)

This thrusts the ball of the foot deeply into the opponent. Practise it from a forward or fighting stance because both have the hip position and weight distribution to allow rapid action. Left fighting stance leads with the left fist at the same height as the shoulder.

Change your guard and turn the right shoulder forward. Lift your right foot clear of the ground and swing the knee forward and up. The supporting leg must be allowed to pivot, bringing your right hip forward. If this isn't done your kick will lose range and power. As your knee rises to point at the target, bring it to a sudden stop and thrust your lower leg into the target. Pull your foot back and set it down carefully.

Gain extra range by dragging your supporting leg forward a short distance, bare instants before the kick strikes home. This action reduces recoil and is useful for lighter students attacking heavier partners.

direct, or in the form of a shallow U, according to your school's teachings. Your hips open out and the reverse punch is cocked, ready for use. As your advancing foot reaches its new position, transfer your weight forward and twist your left hip. Tension builds in your spine and at the optimum moment your left arm thrusts out, its action exactly balanced by your withdrawing right fist.

91

▼ **One-step front kick**
Scissors-step across the front of your supporting leg. Use this as an accelerator

Couple the kick smoothly to the step so that no force is lost

▼ **Roundhouse kick**
▼ *Begin from fighting stance by leaning your upper body away and to the side. Bring your knee up and across*

Thrust out your lower leg when the knee has rotated to the correct position

have an effective guard immediately on hand.

Increase the range of your kick by sliding forward on your supporting leg as your knee reaches the correct height. This adds body weight and makes the kick both more stable and more powerful. Use a scissors step like that in one-step front kick to cover even more distance but make sure you turn your foot outwards, so your hips are set up correctly.

Side kick (*yokogeri*)

This strikes powerfully with the heel and edge of foot. Begin from straddle stance by lifting your front leg, leaning back and shifting your weight over your supporting leg. The kicking knee is raised until the foot is at a correct height to thrust horizontally into the target. Swivel your supporting leg away from the direction of the kick and lean back even more. Pull your knee back to your chest, return to an upright

One-step front kick

Even greater range can be achieved with a step. Begin from either forward or fighting stance, sliding your rear foot forward and turning the toes outwards. Lift your rear foot and accelerate the knee to its correct height. Brake the upper leg to a stop and thrust out the foot, withdraw it, and set it gently down.

Roundhouse kick (*mawashigeri*)

This strikes with either the ball of the foot or the instep. It is called a roundhouse or turning kick because the foot travels in a circular path, first lifting, then curving into the target and travelling parallel to the ground.

Begin practice by twisting your upper body like an aircraft turning and banking away. This pre-loads the spine and charges it with energy. Lift your rear foot off and swivel

on the supporting foot. Accelerate your knee to the correct height, moving it quickly across the front of your body where it acts as a bar against attacks. By now your supporting foot has turned more than 90 degrees and the knee is pointing at the target. Thrust your lower leg out and strike the target, then pull it back to your chest while straightening to an upright position. Set your foot down carefully and ensure you

▼ **Side kick**
Basic side kick is often practised from a straddle stance

Lift your kicking leg from the floor and lean back to counter the weight

Thrust your heel and edge of foot deep into the target. A forward slide on the supporting leg as your kick is extending adds a bonus of power

▼ **One-step side kick**
▼ *This uses scissors step, though on this occasion the advancing foot moves behind the supporting leg. This sets up the hips correctly*

position and set your foot down.

One-step side kick (*surikomi yokogeri*)

This is both fast and powerful. It uses the scissors step with the advancing foot sliding behind the supporting foot. This rotates the hips and sets them up for the kick. Experienced *karateka* simply use a shallow sideways hop, striking with the heel just as weight settles on the new supporting foot.

Back kick (*ushirogeri*)

Practise this kick from left fighting stance, using a strong hip twist to turn your back towards the opponent. Shift weight over your left supporting leg so your right foot is freed to slide in an arc. Maintain guard during and twist your head, so you have a clear view of your opponent. Your body's twisting motion powers the kick, so thrust your foot out while you are turning and not after the turn has stopped. Lift your kicking foot and thrust it into

TRAINING AND TACTICS

Performing a kick correctly involves a lot more than simply raising your leg and letting fly! First you must develop sufficient flexibility in your hip joints, then you must learn how to co-ordinate all the movements so one leads into the next without hesitation. Each element depends on the correct execution of the preceding movement and earlier mistakes often cause a 'knock-on' effect. Control over your centre of gravity is important if you are to recover the spent kick in the shortest possible time.

93

Back kick

1 *Begin from a fighting stance by shifting your weight over the front foot*

2 *Slide your right foot across and look over your shoulder. Keep your arms to your sides*

3 *Thrust your foot heel-first into the target*

the target with your knee facing the ground. Continue to twist your hips, at the same time withdrawing your foot so the knee comes back to your chest. Set it carefully down and turn to face the front once more from an effective fighting stance.

COMBINATION TECHNIQUES

Although a single technique can be effective, in practice an opponent is likely to counter it. It is, of course, much more difficult to cope with several techniques, each coming in from different angles to attack different targets. By means of a sustained attack, the opponent is put under pressure and it only takes one slip for a technique to get through.

Combination techniques link basic moves, whether two basic techniques, or a whole sequence of kicks, punches, blocks and strikes. Some combinations use only hand techniques; others use only the feet, but usually both are combined.

The first technique you use may well influence your choice of the next. For example, a roundhouse kick turns the hips away from the target, so they must twist forward again on landing. What could be more simple than to use this action to thrust out a reverse punch? As you become more skilled, you will instinctively choose the most appropriate follow-up techniques.

▼ **Triple punch**
▼ *Begin with a fast reverse punch to mid-section*

Draw up your rear foot and use back fist to the side of your opponent's head

Step forward and reverse punch to mid-section once more. This switching of targets confuses your opponent

▼ **Snap punch/reverse punch**
Begin from fighting stance, leaning well forward to give the punch maximum range

Use the energy of the withdrawing snap punch to help power a reverse punch to mid-section

Snap punch/reverse punch

This is a useful short combination technique. It is usually referred to as an 'up and under' because it first diverts attention upwards, then bores through under the raised guard to score.

Begin from left fighting stance and make a fast jab at your opponent's face with your leading fist. Lean in slightly to extend range but avoid pushing your chin forward. Even as the snap punch is coming back, thrust your right hip forward and perform a strong reverse punch to the mid-section. If the sequence is fast enough, the opponent is caught out and the second punch scores. Skilled *karateka* punch slightly to the side of the opponent's face to make him shut off his own vision when he blocks.

Triple punch

Next try three punches linked together into a fast, advancing

sequence. Begin from left fighting stance by sliding forward and performing a powerful reverse punch to your opponent's mid-section. Remember to draw up your rear leg so the stance doesn't stretch out unduly.

As soon as the reverse punch is complete, pull back sharply and use this energy to snap out a back fist to the side of your opponent's head. Lean in behind the strike and unroll the arm out from the leading shoul-

der, drawing up the back leg at the same time. Back fist is a long-range technique and its curling action is difficult to block.

Use the hip position and short stance to launch a second reverse punch to mid-section, thrusting forward as you do so.

This is likely to score if you make it follow closely enough on the back fist strike. Note that you advance in three increments, once with each technique.

Front kick/ roundhouse kick
Begin with a front kick to mid-section, dropping the kick in a forward position

Swivel on your leading foot and perform a roundhouse kick to the head. Drop your foot forward after the kick.

guard, just hold your arms firmly but not stiffly to your sides throughout the sequence. Set the kicking foot down carefully in a forward position and immediately lift your left foot. Pivot on the supporting foot and deliver a roundhouse kick to the mid-section. Snap the kick back and set it down. Some people add a reverse punch to the end of the sequence. This isn't a bad move, because the hips must in any case twist forward on landing.

Front kick/roundhouse kick

This is a basic foot combination technique. Practise it from a left fighting stance, using the right leg to front kick to mid-section. Move your hip behind the kick in the normal manner, and snap it back afterwards to prevent it being grabbed. Don't bother changing

Roundhouse kick/ back kick
Begin with a roundhouse kick to the head

Leave your hips turned and drop the spent kick to the floor

Use the pre-set hip position to thrust out a back kick to mid-section

Roundhouse kick/back kick

This uses the twisting motion of a turning kick to set the hips up for a back kick. Begin from left fighting stance and bring your right knee up and forward. Kick to the target and instead of fully withdrawing the foot, allow it to fall to the floor at the correct distance to suit the range. Your hips are turned sideways at this point, so simply turn them completely and thrust out your left foot in a back kick to mid-section.

Front kick/snap punch

This is perhaps the simplest of the hand and foot combinations. Though simple, it is quite effective and uses the weight of the descend-

Front kick/snap punch
Begin with a front kick to mid-section

As weight drops forward, thrust out the rear guard hand in a snap punch to the opponent's face

ing leg to help power the snap punch. Begin from left stance, making a right foot kick with the guard held firmly to the sides. Pull back your left fist as the spent kick touches down and thrust your right out at the same speed. Lean in behind the punch, tucking your chin into your shoulder.

KATA

Kata is a series of combination techniques, performed alone in a standard order, in different directions and at different speeds. It is divided into two categories depending on its Okinawan origins: *shorin* kata originated from the *shurite* and *tomarite* schools and *shorei* kata

from *nahate*. As you might expect, *shorin* kata uses large movements, much agility and hard, focused muscular power whereas *shorei* kata emphasises circular movements and less obvious muscular focus.

Shorin

The most elementary of the *shorin* series is the five training kata called *heians* (peace). These were put together by one of Funakoshi's teachers, Yasutsune Itosu, between 1903 and 1906. Itosu dismembered more advanced *shorin* kata to make a set suitable for teaching to Okinawan school children. *Heians* are also known as *pinans* (peaceful mind) in Okinawa and in the *wado*

ryu. The order in which they are practised is *heian shodan, nidan, sandan, yodan* and *godan*. They become steadily more complicated as one passes from one to the next higher.

Ku shanku/kanku dai Kong Shang Kung, the Chinese military attache to Okinawa, taught the kata *kwanku* (a look towards heaven) to the aptly named 'Karate' Sakugawa and Kitan Yari. They subsequently re-named it *ku shanku*, after the Okinawan reading of his name and this has passed down to the present day, except in shotokan, where it is called *kanku dai* (contemplating the sky). Shotokan practise two versions of this long kata, the first being known as *kanku sho*.

◄ *The bassai dai/passai kata uses a curious double punch which may well be an adaptation from a much earlier form which used a six-foot staff*

▼ *Kata developed from early Okinawan schools of karate*

Seisan/Hangetsu This kata bridges between *shorei* and *shorin* kata. It contains both slow, tense movements performed from *hangetsu-dachi* stance and rapid, snapping techniques more characteristic of shorin systems. Shotokan re-named it *hangetsu* (half moon) because of the semi-circular steps which make up half the performance. Seisan used to be the first kata taught to students, but after 1903 it was replaced by the *pinan* series.

Shorei

Sanchin and tensyo. These are two of the best known *shorei* kata. Both are said to have been originated by Chojun Miyagi, though *sanchin* stance itself owes little to him. *Sanchin* is obviously based on southern *shaolin* forms and it is the core kata of many Okinawan

Chinto/gankaku Another military attache, Chinto, taught a kata which is clearly based on a southern shaolin version of white crane kung fu. It includes several one-legged stances and large movements characteristic of that school. The kata is known as *chinto* (fighting towards the east) except in the shotokan, where it is called *gankaku*, or crane on a rock.

Bassai dai/Passai The kata *bassai* exists as two versions within the shotokan. The first is *bassai sho* and the second *bassai dai*. *Wado ryu* has lost *bassai sho* and practises *bassai dai* under the original name of *passai*. Several other versions are taught in Okinawan schools, the most notable being *tomari-no bassai* and *matsumura-no bassai*.

Wanshu/Enpi This kata teaches a horrifying series of attacks on op-ponents' testicles, in which they are first seized and then torn off! It then defends against a quarterstaff-wielding opponent by grasping the staff with both hands and wrenching it away with a backward-spinning jump. Shotokan has renamed the kata *enpi* (flying swallow).

Unsu This kata teaches one finger spear thrusts and defence from a prone position.

Gojushiho This kata is practised as two versions, both of which use repeated short spearhand strikes. The name means 54 steps.

Niseishi This kata is known also as *niju shiho*. It incorporates a peculiar barring block with the forearm, and a pair of side kicks which follow from powerful grasping and pulling actions.

Tensyo kata is practised with the intention of gaining a yielding resilience to the opponent's force. It is the natural partner of the kata called sanchin

schools. Practice in it leads to great stability and strength of stance.

Tensyo This kata embodies the principles of softness. Its techniques are circular and use less obvious muscular effort, giving the erroneous impression that they are weak. Relaxed techniques can generate a surprising amount of force simply by virtue of the weight of the body weapon chosen and the speed at which it travels. Unfortunately, the core principles of tensyo are nowadays all but lost.

Jutte The name of this *shorei* kata means 'ten hands', from the claim that practice gives one the power of five men.

Jion This kata is named after the Buddhist temple Jion-je.

Seipai This teaches a curious opening sequence using linked hands.

TRAINING AND TACTICS

The first stage in performing a kata is to learn the individual techniques. Then comes the sequences, learning which techniques are linked together into fast movements and which are performed slowly. After a great deal of repetition both these stages become thoroughly established and you no longer need to concentrate on the moves themselves. Your body moves automatically and without prompting. It is only from this point onwards that the art of practising kata can be developed.

Sanseiriu This is an old Okinawan kata common to several schools.

Suparimpei This is the most advanced of the *shorei* kata. It was probably introduced to Okinawan karate during the 19th century by way of Fujian Province on the Chinese mainland. The Chinese characters which make up the name *suparimpei* translated as 108.

Other shorei kata These include *saifa, seyunchin, shisochin, kururunfa* and *naihanchi*. *Naihanchi* uses highly characteristic lateral movements, delivering techniques from a

curious variant of straddle stance in which the knees are forced outwards but the feet converge. Shotokan refers to it as *tekki*, which simply means horse riding.

PRE-ARRANGED SPARRING

Pre-arranged sparring (*yakusoku kumite*) safely teaches the principles of distance and timing, and promotes enthusiastic practice. It is the only method of training for techniques considered too dangerous for free sparring. Your partner knows which techniques you will use, and what responses are scheduled, so injury is less likely.

Begin practice by deciding which of you will open the attack, and who will defend. Either change, then change about, or preferably remain in your role for, say, five repetitions. Strive for realism! The attacker must strongly press home the attack, so you learn how to cope with it. Attack the actual target, and not a point near it.

Begin practice at a speed both of you can handle. If you manage to defend successfully, increase the speed of attack, so you are always put under pressure. If the pressure is too great, however, your response will break up. Therefore co-operate with each other to achieve suitable levels.

The effectiveness of any pre-arranged sparring exercise depends on distance. Adjust this either before or during the exercise, so the attack would actually hit you if you didn't take evasive action. If you stand too close together either the

Five-step sparring
Step back and block the opponent's head punch. Adjust the distance between you by varying the length of your step back

The final move is to reverse punch to mid-section

attack, or the response (or both) may be invalidated. Try using roundhouse kick to the head when you are inside punching range! If you stand too far apart the attack falls short and the planned follow-up gets stretched out of shape.

Begin from fighting stance, the attacker inching forward while you remain stationary. The distance is approximately correct when your forward guards are about 10 cm/ 4 inches apart. Having said that, attacks using kicks may need a little more space.

Your evasion movement must be sufficient for the attack to miss, yet not so great as to make your planned counter-attack fall short.

Respond to an attack at the right time. Too early a response alerts the attacker and in the real world, he will re-direct his attack to your new

position or stance. Too late a response makes you act in haste and perhaps spoils the technique. Aim to identify the incoming attack as soon as possible. This will save you from inadvertently ducking into an upswinging kick, or stepping sideways into the part of a roundhouse kick! If there is any hiccup in the system, then withdraw to a make-safe position.

There are several types of pre-arranged sparring. *Gohon kumite* (five-step sparring) uses five successive and identical attacks. You block four and counter-attack on the fifth. For example, your partner advances, each time performing a lunge punch into your face. You take a full step backward and head block, so the punch is re-directed harmlessly upwards. He attacks with a second punch and you once more retreat a

step and head block. This happens twice more but on the fifth attack, you follow the head block with a reverse punch to his mid-section. Use *kiai* to underline your counter-attack.

This type of pre-arranged sparring is excellent for teaching timing and distance. Repetition of similar attacks provides a dynamic way of training in head block.

Three-step sparring (*sanbon kumite*) is very similar except that the counter is made on the last of three similar attacks. One-step sparring (*ippon kumite*) uses a single attack and an immediate counter. Often, one-step sparring is used to test the validity of actual fighting techniques.

In the next example a front kick is used against a lower parry (*gedan barai*) in a one-step sequence. Begin

One-step sparring
Take a full step back and block your opponent's front kick with gedan barai

Give him no chance to recover. Thrust off your rear foot and perform a reverse punch to mid-section

by stepping back into left fighting stance. Your opponent advances into a left stance, adjusts his distance and performs a front kick to your mid-section. Take a full step back and fold your right arm across your chest. Bring it sharply down into a lower parry, striking the side of your opponent's leg and knocking it outward. Even before the opponent has a chance to collect himself, reverse punch him to mid-section and then take a full step back to fail-safe distance.

Jiu ippon kumite is limited to single, realistic attacks which are agreed beforehand. However, your response can be entirely free. The attacker realistically stalks you and maybe switches stance quickly a number of times, just to throw you. When he is ready, he performs the agreed attack under free-sparring conditions. This means that he uses full speed and aims at the target he wants to reach. Having performed the technique, he withdraws quickly.

FREE SPARRING

Free sparring usually takes place at the end of a training session and in some ways this is a pity because fatigue is setting in and skill level drops. Ideally, your partner will be roughly the same build as you, though it does not matter whether he is a higher grade. In fact it is safer to train with higher grades because they can control their techniques and are less likely to cause inadvertent injury.

Large students can't help developing a lot of power, even when they move relatively slowly. There-fore be careful when blocking their techniques and try for evasions rather than direct counters.

Always control the force you put into your techniques and if you haven't yet mastered a technique, don't use it! Do not attack the opponent's instep, ankle, shin, knee, or groin. Close your hands into properly formed fists when attacking the face. Loose fingers and thumbs can so easily catch the eye. Take care when blocking kicks, because a limp wrist or open fingers are soon injured by a hard shin bone. Many facial injuries occur when the opponent runs onto, or ducks into a technique, so bear this in mind.

Sparring at reduced speed is a valuable exercise for teaching skills. It is far from easy to do, yet it is less frightening. Remember though,

In free sparring it is not so hard to hurt your partner. Controlling impact, however, requires a much higher order of skill

that the techniques are travelling slowly, so you shouldn't take unfair advantage by, for example, grabbing hold of a kick.

COMPETITION

Sparring competition is a form of free sparring in which half- or full-point scores are awarded. The following description has been taken from the rules of the world karate governing body.

Arena

Sparring competitions are held on 8-metre squares and your techniques will only score while you remain inside the area boundary. Having said that, you can score on an opponent who steps out, as long as you do so before the referee calls a halt.

Teams

Team reserves can be used at the discretion of the team manager and before each match he hands in to the scorekeeper a list of team members in the order they will fight. Once handed in, this order is fixed and any departure from it will result

in the team's disqualification from that match. Also, once handed in, the fighting order stands until superseded in a subsequent round. Male teams are only allowed to compete if they can field a minimum of three fighters. Female teams require at least two fighters. Absent teams are given a short time to assemble at the area, after which time they lose by what is called a 'no-show'.

Timing

Sparring competition is held in team or individual categories and senior male bouts last three minutes. All other bouts last two minutes.

Scoring

The maximum score in a bout is three points, made up of full points (*ippons*) and half-points (*waza-ari*), but the total number of both cannot exceed a three-point maximum score.

A full point is awarded for a technique which has impeccable form, is correctly timed so it strikes the target with maximum effect at the correct distance. Even if your technique lacks that standard of

excellence, you can still get a full point if other factors count in its favour.

The scoring areas of the body are the face, the head, the neck, the chest, the stomach and the back. Teams win when they take more bout victories than their opponents. When bout victories are equal in team contests the total number of points scored determines the winner. If points are equal coaches select a fighter to represent them in a special tie-breaker bout.

Penalties

Close attention is paid to the level of face contact. The referee must assess the impact force and will always take into account the way both parties were moving when the contact was made. He will ask himself 'Did the injured contestant move into the force of the technique and make it worse?'

Penalties are given for prohibited behaviour. These are imposed in the form of a warning, a half-point penalty, a full-point penalty, or for more serious infringements, disqualifications from the match, or even disbarment from the tournament.

A doctor is called on to the area when the referee suspects that injury has been caused and tells the referee whether you may continue.

Appeals

If you are unfairly treated, your coach or a colleague can make a written protest to the arbitrator.

KENJUTSU AND KENDO

Kenjutsu is the Japanese art of using the sword and from it developed kendo, the way of using the sword. Kenjutsu forms a part of the classical Japanese *bujutsu* while kendo is nowadays considered to be a part of classical *budo*.

Although the Japanese sword is generally considered to be the most noble weapon in the classical warrior's armoury, it was not always so. Until the 12th century warriors were publicly praised for their skilful archery but not for prowess with the sword. The names of many famous archers have been passed down from that period, but no great early swordsmen are known to us. This, however, changed with the 1259 edict of Shogun Hojo Tokiyori which restricted the carrying of swords to court nobles and members of the warrior caste only. From that time onwards the sword became the badge of the warrior and supplanted the bow as the most noble weapon.

THE JAPANESE SWORD

The Japanese sword represented the soul of the warrior and as such was venerated and cherished throughout its long life. Swords were believed to possess a life of their own and some were regarded as lucky and others as unlucky, bringing misery and poverty. The Japanese warrior ethic demanded that the sword should never be used with anger or malice. Its sole purpose was the eradication of evil; the cutting out of a malignancy by a dispassionate surgical operation.

Before the 10th century swords were straight and single-edged; it was after this time that the familiar curved design was introduced. The finest quality swords are reckoned to have been made during the Kamakura period (1185–1333), at the time of wars between preeminent clans like the Minamoto and Taira, a good time indeed for the testing of swords.

When the Mongols invaded in 1274 and 1281, a weakness in sword design was discovered: the tip was particularly vulnerable to the chain mail worn by the invaders and snapped off, also destroying the cutting power of the blade. Goro Myudo Masamune eliminated this by tempering and sharpening the blade all in one; previously the tip was hardened and treated separately, causing lines of weakness to develop. Masamune's discovery was sought by all Japan's leading sword makers and such was the originator's pride that he never autographed his blades, believing that

◄ *Kenjutsu is the art of using the live blade. Because of the dangers inherent in practice, each move must be carefully pre-arranged*

Training is provided by means of the kata. Each school of kenjutsu practised its own syllabus of kata

their quality would identify him!

In the Nambokucho era (1336–1392) a split in royal succession resulted in a bitter feud between the Northern and Southern Emperors. During this time the longsword, or *tachi*, was replaced by the shorter and lighter *katana*. The *tachi* was a particularly heavy weapon, slung from the left hip and worn with the cutting edge downwards, to facilitate its use by mounted warriors. However, it was rather unwieldy and needed considerable strength and sword-fighting skill to be effective. Fighting with a *tachi* involved powerful circular cuts which, because of the blade's weight, acquired considerable momentum and made for rather crude techniques. Dismounted warriors preferred to use a two-handed grip because of the better control this gave. Though the sword's weight made handling difficult, it could cut through armour very effectively.

The *katana*, by comparison, was pushed through the belt, with the cutting edge uppermost. This lighter weapon enabled new techniques to be used which were subsequently incorporated into the martial traditions of ken jutsu and iai jutsu.

Korean metalworkers brought to Japan during the late 16th century used the principle of compression forging to produce a dense steel that was far harder and more resilient than earlier materials.

HISTORY

The chapter on Japanese *bujutsu ryu* explains how a core of practical knowledge of weapons use grew up. Briefly, a warrior of proven ability taught his techniques to other members of the school in which he trained. These schools existed from earliest times but the earliest that can be historically verified is the *nen ryu* of Yoshimoto Sanashiro, which was founded in 1350. Some swordmasters worked for a feudal lord and others wandered the country and taught those who wished to learn from them. Perhaps the most famous of these was Tsukahara Bokuden (1490–1571), a swordmaster who travelled with a retinue of more than a hundred men.

Swordsmen wishing to test their ability issued challenges to known masters. If the challenge was accepted, the two met and fought with real weapons. Other duels were fought as a result of family feuds, or as matters of honour. It was enough merely to brush someone's scabbarded sword for a duel to result and some warriors wore their longswords in such a way as to make such contact almost inevitable. Not only were other warriors fair game for attack: unarmed men and women could also expect to be struck down for the same insult.

Training to use the sword properly meant practising with the live blade. Obviously this was extremely hazardous and so forms of practice were devised in which each move was carefully planned. These were called kata and each one focused on a particular series of techniques. It is recorded that of the 200 or so schools practising during the 18th

▼ *The oaken sword was hardly less lethal than the live blade!*

The kendo headguard permits hard, yet safe training. Previously all practice was with the live blade. Later the equally lethal oaken sword came to be used more frequently

century the *ono ha itto ryu* alone practised more than 100 katas!

In the search for greater realism of practice, the wooden sword, or *bokuto*, was developed. This allowed two people to train with techniques previously too dangerous with live blades. It is, however, important to note that training with the *bokuto* in no way replaced kata. Both forms of practice were necessary if the warrior wanted the maximum benefit. The *bokuto* came to be used more in duels, reducing

fatalities, although the *bokuto* was itself potentially a lethal weapon. The famous swordsman Miyamoto Musashi (1584–1645) killed many people with his *bokuto*.

Because the oak sword was less likely to kill or maim, it appears that many warriors grew a little careless during practice, not bothering much to control the level of contact, resulting in bloody heads and badly bruised arms. Armour was introduced during the Edo period (1615–1868) in the form of a padded iron-grid mask, a breastplate made from bamboo strips sewn into tough cloth, forearm/wrist protectors of a similar construction and a padded apron. This changed in the early 19th century, when gauntlets

▼ *The modern kendoka wears a headguard, throat protector, breastplate and padded gauntlets*

KENJUTSU THEN AND NOW

Kenjutsu is the oldest of the Japanese martial art traditions. More than 200 different schools flourished during the 18th century. It is based on the use of the sword, though a small amount of grappling was also taught for use in close-quarter engagement. Practice originally involved use of the live blade, though the oak sword was introduced later. A headguard and armour allowed powerful cuts to be made. The introduction of firearms made it possible for a conscript army to defeat a force of skilfull swordsmen and from then on the art of the sword became a way of increasing fighting spirit.

replaced the wrist/forearm protectors and the breastplate became a wrap-around padded jacket. Modern armour has replaced the padded jacket with a curved and solid breastplate that extends back to cover the ribs. The *bokuto* was replaced by the much lighter bamboo *shinai*, which made even faster strikes possible.

As the Edo period drew towards its close it became evident that the sword was no longer a valid military weapon. In 1876 an edict called for the setting aside of the sword but a year later the rebellious Satsuma clan rose up, only to be annihilated by a conscript army using firearms. Their sacrifice was not wholly in vain because it clearly showed the government the value of martial spirit. From that time on the decline in old martial art practice was halted and

training was introduced into schools and colleges. In 1912 the various schools of kendo came together and agreed a set of rules for competition in armour and with the bamboo sword.

PRESENT-DAY PRACTICE

Kendo practice takes place in the *dojo*, or 'place of training in the way'. Those who practise kendo – *kendoka* – are required to behave politely, bowing on entering and leaving the *dojo*, and showing respect to the teacher and other students. Fencing equipment consists of the *shinai*, the mask (*men*), breastplate (*do*), padded apron (*tare*) and gauntlets (*kote*). Kendo uniform consists of a jacket (*kendo-gi*), wide trousers (*hakama*) and a head towel (*tenugui*).

▼ Kendo armour consists of a headguard, breastplate and gauntlets. The practice sword is made from strips of bamboo

▼ The throat is
▼ attacked with a powerful thrust

Opening moves
1 The kendoka sinks down on to his haunches and draws his shinai

2 Returning to his feet, the kendoka takes up the middle guard position in preparation to spar

▼ The most common
▼ attack is to the head. The headguard permits full-power strikes to be made

1

2

The *kendoka* dons his equipment and finds a partner to practise with. They stand facing each other, about 3 metres/yards apart, holding the *shinais* in their left hands. The left thumb locks over the finger guard. Moving in unison, both sink to their

A cut to the opponent's mid-section is made the instant he raises his shinai to a high position

The shoulder position is used for cutting the opponent's wrist

haunches while withdrawing the *shinais*. The right hand grips the *shinai* just below the finger guard and the left grips the lower part. Both partners then stand and each steps back a half-pace with the left leg. The *shinai* lies in the middle position (*chudan kamae*), with its point at chest height.

Weight is distributed evenly on the feet, so movement can be made quickly in any direction. The feet skim over the ground and distance is adjusted either by stepping, or by taking a half-pace forward with the right foot, then closing up with the left. When moving backward, the left foot draws back first and the front follows. The correct distance between fencers is when the tips of their *shinais* are just crossing.

The scoring areas of the head, arms and body are struck with a cutting action (*kiri*), except for the throat, which is attacked by a straight thrust (*tsuki*). Cuts to the head are the most frequently used technique. They are made by raising the sword above the head and then bringing it sharply down, using the shoulders as pivots. The left hand brings the sword down and the right directs it. As the sword passes vertical, the slightly bent elbows are straightened and as impact is about to be made, the right hand grips tightly in a spasm action. As the cut is made, the *kendoka* emits a piercing shout. This is known as the *kiai* and it signifies resolve to strike strongly.

Whenever the opponent raises his *shinai* to a high position, he exposes his mid-section to attack. The defender holds his shinai in the *katsugi*, or shoulder position, because this makes for a shorter and faster movement. Sliding the left hand up to the right during the cut provides extra acceleration. The opponent's wrist will become vulnerable if his sword is held at a slight angle. The defender pulls back his sword from *chudan kamae* to an upright position, then he glides forward and cuts across the exposed wrist.

Thrusts are made with the hands twisting inwards, or outwards during execution. Most of the force is developed by sliding forward with stiffened elbows. The thrust either drives diagonally upwards into the throat, or it travels horizontally.

KOBUJUTSU AND KOBUDO

K obujutsu and Kobudo are Japanese terms, respectively meaning 'old martial arts' and 'old martial ways'. Nowadays, the general use of the terms kobujutsu and kobudo has narrowed down to cover unusual weapons. To avoid duplicating what has already been said in earlier chapters, this account will concern itself only with Okinawan kobudo and kobujutsu.

HISTORY

Until the early 17th century, when Okinawa was annexed by the mainland Japanese, it had its own series of military arts, blended from indigenous Chinese and Japanese systems. Unarmed and covertly armed fighting systems were unusually prevalent because in 1470 a royal edict forbade weapons to other than the king's officers. Without an effective police force to protect

Pairs of sai *are used together in training kata. They are used* *to trap, block, stab and bludgeon*

them, the peasants were obliged to use agricultural and domestic implements as weapons. Once the Japanese had established themselves as overlords, all Okinawan martial art practice by members of the indigenous military caste was stopped. Few Okinawan nobles would 'stoop' to train in covertly armed non-military systems, so this line of development ceased.

Five covert weapons were employed and training methods sprang up to promote their effective use. These methods all included unarmed combat and it is interesting to note that while training with the weapons has virtually died out, the unarmed portion survives today as karate. The five covert weapons were the staff, the forked truncheon, the sickle, the rice grinder handles and the rice flails. None of these were indigenous to Okinawa but were introduced through cultural interchange, for Okinawa was on an important trading route.

The staff, or rokushakubo, was nearly 2 metres/6 feet long and made of polished, hard wood and sometimes tapered from the centre to both ends. While the Japanese staff was swung in vicious arcs, the Okinawan staff was used to extend the body's natural weapons, giving extra range to punches, a rigid bar for blocks, providing leverage for joint locks and occasionally leverage for throws. Its size made it difficult to use in enclosed spaces.

Many training sequences, or kata, were devised to familiarise users with the weapon's characteristics.

Some of these passed into modern-day karate without the staff and as a result, a great many applications of moves in kata are now completely misunderstood.

The forked truncheon, or sai, was a metal bludgeon with two curving and smaller tines. The butt end of the truncheon was used to club down the opponent. The other end was pointed and with a little practice, the *sai* could be thrown at a target. Its weight gave it good penetration. The tines functioned as finger guards and it is said that a sword blade trapped between them could be shattered by twisting the *sai*.

Training kata used pairs of *sai* in combination with kicks and evasive movements. Each *sai* was held near its point of balance, so it could be quickly flipped over from butt-facing to point forward. With the butt end facing, a punch was extended and impact made more severe. With the point facing, a jab could drive it through muscle. Laid along the forearm, it would protect flesh from swings with a staff and even, it was claimed, a sword! Pairs of *sai* were also used in x-block configurations, to trap an opponent's weapon.

The sickle, or kama, was a legitimate farmer's implement and was also used for killing the dangerous Okinawan viper. It was equally effective against human aggressors, being used in pairs to cut, stab, or club the opponent. The sickle is usually held by the butt, with the

Okinawan sickles are used in pairs, normally with the blades facing forward

▼ The rice flail is difficult to use and requires a lot of practice before it can be used safely

Pairs of tonfa extend the punch and provide additional rigidity to the blocking forearm. They can also be swung around and into the target

curved, heavy blade pointing forward. In this position it can chop at hands holding weapons, or stab into flesh. Sometimes the batons were twisted so as to run along the forearms, with the blades projecting outwards. Used in this way, an elbow strike became a fearsome short-range weapon. For less deadly attacks, the blade could be turned backwards and the baton used to club the opponent.

Rice grinder handles, or tonfa,

were interesting domestic implements which, with a little training, became formidable weapons. They consisted of a flattened, heavy wood baton with a peg projecting at right angles near one end. These too were used in pairs. With the longer part of the baton lying against the forearm, the butt end projected forward and the hand grasped the peg. The butt gave extension and force to a punch, and the baton protected the forearm from injury. Held this way, the *tonfa* was swung out in a circle towards the opponent and as it neared him, forward motion suddenly stopped. This flipped the baton forward and into a strike to the side of the opponent's head. Interestingly a modern version of the *tonfa* has been taken up by American police forces because it has been found to be more effective than the orthodox truncheon.

The rice flail, or nun chaku, is

perhaps the most famous of all the Okinawan covert weapons. Originally flails were simply heavy, flat batons linked by a leather hinge. Converted flails used a universal joint of cord or metal link, their batons were of round or octagonal section and made of dense wood. They were used in a variety of ways, the simplest being to hold both batons in one hand to club the opponent. More common was the practice of holding one baton and swinging the other in wide, fast arcs. Used in this way, the rice flail becomes a potentially lethal weapon. Occasionally, the thong was slipped around the opponent's throat and the batons crossed behind his neck, making an effective garotte.

Rice flail training katas taught how to control the swinging baton, transferring it smoothly from hand to hand as it wove a wall of wood around the user, through which nothing could pass.

KUNG FU

Kung fu is a Chinese term meaning well done. It is analogous to bujutsu in the Japanese military tradition, an umbrella term for any activity used in waging war. Therefore it includes classical weapon training using the sword, spear, bow and arrow, work with the quarterstaff, rice flails etc., and an element of unarmed combat. The unarmed element has increased enormously and in many schools the original weapon practices have all but died out. The mainland's *wu shu* does, however, preserve weapon forms on an equal footing with unarmed combat.

Kung fu may be classified in many different ways: whether weapons are used or not or whether the bulk of its practice involves grappling or striking techniques. By far the larger of the two is striking systems, which can be divided according to whether they use punches which travel the full length of the arm — long-hand boxing, or whether they travel only very short distances — short-hand boxing. Both divisions may be further broken down according to whether the techniques are applied with great muscular effort, in which case they are said to be external. If little apparent

Mainland China's wu shu *practice uses training patterns which employ traditional weapons*

▼ The sword is used in many classical kung fu systems

▶ The term 'kung fu' is used to describe an entire range of martial technique, from weapon-using systems to empty-hand methods

muscular exertion is used, then they are said to be internal. A further broad division is marked by the Yangtse River: northern schools use large, circular movements, high kicks and agile, jumping techniques whereas southern techniques tend to be short-range, use short movements and have no high kicks.

Martial arts practice in China extends back into the remote past and the earliest reference to it is found in the Chou Dynasty (1122-255 BC). Additional sources mention military demonstrations given by the sons of the nobility. These included archery,

riding, sword-fighting and wrestling. Wrestling was of a combat type, rather than the combat sport seen today.

There was a flowering of martial art techniques during the Ming Dynasty (1368–1644) but when the Manchus invaded during the following Ching Dynasty (1644-1911), thousands of loyal martial artists joined secret societies dedicated to restoring the previous rule. This aim was never achieved.

The Republic of China was inau-

▼ *Tai chi chuan uses relaxed movements to generate considerable power*

► *Choy lay fut kung fu uses the full length of the arm in powerful, swinging strikes*

▼ *Tai chi chuan uses relaxed movements to generate considerable power*

► *Choy lay fut kung fu uses the full length of the arm in powerful, swinging strikes*

gurated in 1912 and the military traditions (*wu shu*) were renamed national art, or *kuoshu*. The rise to power of the Communists drove many martial artists to withdraw to Taiwan, with the defeated forces of General Chiang Kai-shek. Others escaped to Hong Kong, where they formed the nucleus of present-day practice.

No description of the Chinese martial arts is complete without mention of the famous Shaolin su Buddhist Monastery. This exists today at the northern foot of the Sungshan mountains, in the north-western part of T'eng Feng district in the Honan province of China. The monastery was built in AD 496, during the reign of Emperor Hsiao Wen (471-500) of the northern Wei dynasty.

The monastery was burned down

in 535 as the wars between the north and the south raged but it was rebuilt in the reign of Sui Wen-ti and given the name Chihu su, meaning 'ascending the hill'. The name changed to Shaolin during the Tang Dynasty (618-960). One of the monastery's most famous visitors was the Indian Zen Buddhist monk Bodidharma (Ta Mo in Chinese). Bodidharma taught the importance of formal meditation as a way of achieving the enlightenment sought by all Buddhists. During this activity the mind lets go of all thoughts, turning inwards on itself in the expectation of returning to a state of clear perception. However, sitting in meditation for several hours each day will not equip the monk to work hard in the monastery, so some form of physical exercise was necessary. It is claimed that Bodidharma taught

martial art to the monks but this is a historically unsupported assertion.

Whether he did or not is of academic interest only, for the monastery grew in reputation as a result of the fighting skill and martial spirit of its monks. The monastery supported Li Shih-min against the usurper Wang Shih-chung and when Li was made Emperor T'sai Tung, he gave the monastery extensive grants of land and privileges.

The monastery continued to develop during the Ming Dynasty (1368-1644), sending warriors to combat the Japanese invaders. In 1674 a force of warrior monks went to the aid of Emperor Kang and when they had done their duty, he burned down the monastery for the second time in its long history. The monks were scattered and legend has it that only five survived. These

The staff is a traditional weapon of the Chinese warrior monk. It is said that the best staff techniques were taught at the Shaolin Temple

are referred to as the Five Ancestors and it is claimed that all subsequent shaolin teachings have been passed down through them. The monastery's status began to decline when the military situation changed, and China came under the influence of Western nations. It was burned down again during the early 20th century and its monks scattered but they later returned to help make it habitable once more. The Cultural Revolution halted progress for a time but it has now resumed and the monastery functions as a museum, attended by a small number of monks. The famous wall mural which shows monks training in martial art remains unharmed.

Not all Buddhist monks are attached to monasteries. Many received their training and then wandered through China, teaching martial art as they went. Some were great observers and picked up new techniques to add to their core of knowledge. Others originated their own variations until the original shaolin teaching had been much reworked. The students they taught also added their own variations, keeping these secret except to members of their own families. This is where the name 'family style' originates. The secrecy inherent in their teachings makes it impossible to say with any degree of certainty how many forms of kung fu there currently are.

The monks were, of course, unarmed except for a staff, and their teachings sometimes omitted training with military weapons. These schools must be distinguished from the full-blown military traditions also found at that time. The former systems were taught to peasants, farmers and merchants; the latter to the military caste.

Shaolin techniques were hard, using a great amount of muscle power, which did not suit everyone. The Taoist schools had developed a form of fighting which did not use much muscular effort. These were the internal systems, which used

▼ Tai chi chuan is considered by many to be the ultimate form of unarmed Chinese martial art

▶ Tai chi techniques are performed in a slow, relaxed fashion

fast but relaxed movements to generate power. Central to their teachings was the notion of *chi*, a vital force which flows through the body and invigorates it. Internal training tried to harness *chi*, increasing its production and channelling it to produce powerful techniques.

KUNG FU SYSTEMS

There are three major systems of internal kung fu. These are *Hsing ye*, or 'mind boxing', *pa qua* or 'eight trigrams' and *tai chi chuan*, meaning 'great ultimate fist'.

Hsing ye

This is regarded as the least sophisticated of the three and its movements appear similar to those used in the hard schools, although there is no spasm action of the muscles during the generation of impact power.

Pa kua

This is said to have based its practice on the Chinese method of divination known as the *I Ching*, which tries to discern recognised patterns – or trigrams – created by dried yarrow stalks which have been cast on a mat.

Tai chi chuan

This is considered the most sophisticated of the three, though the way it is normally practised would not give this impression. When practised at speed, *tai chi chuan* is an effective fighting system.

117

true, *wing chun kuen* does not use great force in the execution of its techniques. Though some exponents do seem to use a lot of power, traditionally the style is a soft one. It is also noted for the short distance that its punches and strikes travel. *Wing chun kuen* is a close-range system of unarmed self-defence. It has one of the smallest syllabuses of any martial art system and it is probably one of the most scientific.

It would be wrong to give the impression that the martial arts were either entirely hard, or entirely soft: each contains elements of the other to a greater or lesser extent.

Tai chi chuan training takes the form of slow, rhythmic movements combined together into training forms. The exercise of these movements is claimed to help generate and direct *chi*. Pair-form practice takes the form of 'pushing hands', where the partners try to sense each other's flow of *chi*. Less charitable critics have suggested that *tai chi chuan* is an old person's art, to be practised when the body has lost its strength with age, and it does indeed allow the older martial artist to continue training. His great skill, earned over years of practice, will enable him to use many short cuts of technique perhaps not available to younger participants.

Wing chun kuen

This southern system is one of the most popular styles of kung fu practised today. It is named after a young woman who learned it from a Buddhist nun named Ng Mui. As you might expect, if this tradition is

1 *The Tiger is perhaps the best known of all the animal styles. Its techniques rely on external power, so it falls into the 'hard' classification of Kung fu*

2 *The Tiger stylist uses jolting palm-heel thrusts and clawing hand strikes made in a short downwards arc. Typically the arms move together to ensure a balanced delivery*

3 *Shaolin styles use great agility and strength, so supplementary training routines are essential. These are based on traditional methods and train the body in exactly the right way*

4 *The Dragon moves straight into the opponent. He uses his hands like tearing grabs to seize the opponent in a vice-like grip. Circular blocking techniques are followed by straight strikes*

5 *The Crane uses light, expansive and agile movements to evade the opponent's attack. Nevertheless, the Crane stylist remains close by so he can use light, fast strikes*

6 *Hand movements simulate the action of the crane's beak. What they lack in power, they make up for with accurate targeting. The body is poised and ready for rapid movement*

THE FIVE ANIMALS

Many systems of Chinese martial art are founded on the movements of five animals, the tiger, leopard, dragon, snake and crane. Animals feature prominently in Chinese martial art and in the Han dynasty (AD 25-220), the physician Hua To developed a series of fitness exercises based on the movements of the deer, tiger, bear, monkey and bird. The systems don't simply copy the action of these particular animals but rather look for correspondences, taking the essence of each animal's nature as a model.

The Tiger

This is perhaps the best known of all the Five Animal systems. It embodies external strength and agility, using as its principal weapons palm-heel strikes and claw-hand delivered with a short downwards arc. Each movement is paralleled with an opposite movement of your unused arm, thus ensuring a balanced delivery. Evasive movements keep your body close to your opponent while deflecting his attacks. Blocks make use of the palm-heel, or the forearm. Favoured targets for attack are the face and neck, the inner part of the upper arm, the ribs, groin and stomach.

The opponent is caught in a steely grip that digs claw-like into his arms; then the vital points are attacked, paralysing large areas of his body. To develop the fierce grip needed, a small canvas bag contain-

1

2

3

4

5

6

1 *Kung fu stances reflect the underlying theories used by a particular school. An expert can tell which school an exponent belongs to solely from the appearance of a stance*

2 *The Leopard lies mid-way between the Dragon and the Tiger. He uses a characteristic one-knuckle punch to attack the opponent's vital parts*

3 *The Snake appears to use less muscular power than the other animal styles. This is because it relies on the generation of internal power. Its principal weapon is the fingertips*

4 *Snake stylists use sinuous, coiled movements to deliver fast strikes to the opponent's eyes, temple, throat, groin and solar plexus. The opponent's force is re-directed and used against him*

5 *By way of comparison, Southern Shaolin styles use compact stances, shorter movements and fewer high kicks. They played a major role in the development of Okinawan martial arts*

6 *Northern Shaolin styles use long stances, expansive movements and high kicks. They are said to originate from north of the Yangtse River. They may have influenced the Korean martial arts*

ing lead shot is thrown into the air and snatched with a downwards grasp or upwards plucking movement.

The Dragon

The Dragon stylist uses a powerful and direct advance straight into the opponent. His hands reach out like grabs, seizing the opponent in a powerful grip. If the opponent has the initiative, the Dragon fighter will step diagonally forwards and to the side, using circular blocks combined with straight strikes. Dragon fist is an orthodox punch using the three joints of the middle, ring and little finger and delivered with the elbow pointing downwards.

Dragon training exercises work the movement of the wrist and lower forearm – the elbow joint is not used. A jar filled with sand or lead shot until it weighs about 1 kilo is rotated from side to side in the fingers. This produces a fearsome grip and great strength in the forearms.

The Leopard

Leopard lies mid-way between the Dragon and Tiger, advancing like a Dragon but striking like the Tiger with palm-heel or a characteristic one-knuckle punch. Open-hand strikes are quite common and the stiffened fingers are used either to attack vital points or to seize limbs. Some strikes are circular, curling around the opponent's blocking arm to hit the target. The guard uses hands at different heights, one

'Sticking hands' 1
1 *Begin by resting your left fist on your partner's right block*

2 *Follow his arm as it drops, curling your wrist over his forearm*

3 *Thrust downwards on your partner's arm, preventing him from striking you in the chest*

4 *Then punch to his face. The opponent senses your movement and rolls his forearm up to block it. The cycle then repeats*

held high and forwards, the other low and in front of the groin.

The Crane

This is a far more open style, relying on large movements, as often circular as direct. Attacks are characteristically made with the pursed fingers and blocks use the back of the wrist or an open-handed slap. The Crane stylist is agile, preferring to give ground tactically rather than stand toe to toe. Opening advances are fast but not carried all the way through.

The Snake

The Snake relies on internal power and therefore appears less forceful than the other styles. The fingertips are the Snake's main weapons and are hardened by repeatedly driving them into sand. Targets for strikes are the temples, eyes, throat, armpit, solar plexus and groin. Both arms move in synchrony such that they entrap the opponent's strikes and kicks. There is no direct meeting of force against force; rather the opponent's attack is re-directed and the surplus energy used against him.

TRAINING

Working at extremely close range gives little time to decide what the opponent is doing, and then to respond to it. This therefore calls for a system in which the opponent's moves are sensed. 'Sticking hands' is an accurate description of the

form which training takes. It relies on maintaining close contact with the opponent's arms and sensing his intent. There is a comparatively small number of combination deflections/strikes and these are repeatedly practised until they can be performed very quickly indeed. One of these combinations is used as soon as a weakness is felt.

The following are two examples which you can practise with a partner. Stand facing each other in a

straddle stance. Extend your right arm and make a fist, drawing the left back to your ribs. You should be able to touch the centre of his chest with your fist. Move until range is correct. Your partner raises his left arm, bending it at the elbow, so the forearm pushes up your punch and his fingers project into the centre-line of his own body. He pulls his right fist back to his side.

Let your punch lie passively on top of his blocking forearm and you

'Sticking hands' 2
1 Block your partner's face punch with a rolling block

2 Seize his wrist with your left hand and pull it downwards

3 Strike to his face through the gap you have made

4 He blocks your punch with a rolling block and pulls it downwards

5 He then strikes through the gap he has made, but you deflect his punch with a rolling block to begin the sequence once more

will feel it move as he drops it straight down and twists it palm-upwards facing. As it drops, un-clench your fist and curl the fingers and palm over his wrist. Your opponent then twists his palm forward and tries to thrust his palm-heel into your chest. As he does so, your resting right hand detects the movement and you thrust it downwards. Turn your fingers upwards as you do and make the downwards deflection a crisp action. His thrust is taken harmlessly downwards and

you immediately use your right hand to thrust at his chest with a punch.

His deflected hand remains in contact with your forearm and even as it rises, he follows the movement. As your fist extends, his elbow bends and rises into the opening block, and your punch is harmlessly re-directed upwards again. Repeat this sequence several times, then change hands.

The second sequence begins with your partner extending his left fist towards your face. His right hand is held open and waiting near the crook of his left elbow. You deflect the punch with an upwards-rolling action of your right forearm, raising your left hand and bringing it into the mid-line of your body. Seize his left fist with your left hand and pull it down to your blocking forearm. Roll your right arm around and strike at his face with a back fist. He responds by raising his left elbow into a rising block, thus deflecting your strike. Moving quickly, he grasps your right fist in his right arm and pulls it down along his forearm.

As you release your left hand and bring it back into an open guard position, he attempts back fist strike into your face with his freed left fist. You respond by blocking upwards with your right arm and the next sequence begins.

Both these are simple one-handed techniques. Later both hands are used in a rolling movement as the partners circle, or move back and forward.

KYUDO

HISTORY

Many different and diverse qualities went to produce a master archer, skilled in the techniques of Japanese archery, or *kyu jutsu*. These included clear vision and accurate depth perception, the strength to draw the heavy bow, and a firmness of resolve which allowed an accurate release of the arrow towards its target. This resolve was further divided into actually aiming at the target (*monomi*) and then keeping a steady sight (*mikomi*).

The story of Arjuna, a well-known archer, is used to illustrate the concept of aiming: while competing at a tournament, archers were asked what the target was and all except Arjuna answered that it was a painting of a fish set high on a pole, but Arjuna replied: 'The eye of the fish'. He won the tournament.

The good archer was able to widen and narrow his field of concentration selectively so as to zero-in on the selected target while also being aware of other activities beyond this pinpoint which might affect accurate targeting. This combined form of perception was enhanced through a study of Zen Buddhism.

Once a state of what is called 'no mind' has been achieved through Buddhist practices, it became possible to release arrows calmly at selected targets despite being in a confused and dangerous melee.

THE JAPANESE BOW

This is unevenly curved, with the grip nearer one end than the other,

The Way of the Bow cultivates the martial spirit needed for effective combat in the midst of a pitched battle

◀ The bow was once regarded as the most noble weapon in the Japanese warrior's armoury

▼ The archer takes two arrows from the quiver and nocks one of them

He raises the bow above his head in the action known as uchiokoshi

which allowed the bow to be used on horseback, switching from side to side of the horse's neck without snagging the saddle. Despite its asymmetry, the bow drew evenly, thanks to its composite construction from layers of bamboo glued together. Thickness of the laths and the number used determined the pull and range of the bow. The bowstring too is composite, several strands being glued together until it is thick enough to fit snugly into the arrow's nock.

Though archery was eventually superseded on the battlefield by musketry, it was not totally discarded and became changed into the *kyu do* ('way of the bow'), in which form it is practised today.

PRESENT-DAY PRACTICE

Each kyudo practice session begins with a period of seated meditation, or *za zen*. Next the target is saluted by groups of archers advancing on the target with lowered bows, using a peculiar sliding motion of the feet over the polished wooden floor of the training hall. When this ritual is completed, the practice proper begins.

Arrows are kept together in a free-standing quiver from which the archer draws two. He then addresses the target, dropping smoothly to one knee and nocking the arrow while holding the bow well out from the body. Rising smoothly to a standing position, he spreads his feet to more than a shoulder width

1,2 *The bow is part-way drawn by a pushing action of the left arm*

3,4 *The bow is fully drawn and the archer sights on the target*

5 *Arrow release is spontaneous, occurring when the mind and body have achieved unity*

and turns them so they face outwards. He stands sideways-on, keeping his head perfectly upright and turned towards the target. The elbows are held out from the body, the left hand gripping the bow and the right holding the nocked arrow. This is known as *yugamae*.

Next the bow is raised in the action known as *uchiokoshi*. The arms straighten and the bow and arrow are lifted upwards, while keeping the shoulders relaxed and low. The arrow and line of sight to the target are perfectly parallel. At full lift the straightened arms are held up and out 45 degrees from the horizontal. Then the bow is drawn, beginning with a pushing action of the left hand which takes up a third of the pull. This is known as *daisin*, the great third. The bow is gradually lowered and using elbow action, the right hand draws the bowstring back to full tension in the act of *hikiwake*.

The arrow is now held at the level of the chin and lies parallel with the shoulder blades. The eyes sight along the line of the extended left index finger and the whole body settles into a state of unity with the mind. Arrow release (*hanare*) is not conscious but spontaneous, happening when the mind and body have achieved a state of perfect unity. The bow is allowed to rotate in the grip and the mind remains attentive even after the arrow is released. Posture is retained with the left arm still fully extended and the right withdrawn. This is known as *zanshin*.

1

2

TRAINING AND TACTICS

If you have to concentrate on getting correct form you have not yet mastered the way of the bow. First learn the individual components, then practise them until they become second nature. Then forget them and practise with a tranquil mind.

3

4

5

NINJUTSU

HISTORY

Under the feudal military government of Japan, known as the Tokugawa Shogunate, overt acts of warfare between rival lords were frowned on. The climate was therefore ripe for using mercenaries who, if they were caught, could not be traced back to any particular employer.

The idea of covert warriors, as distinct from mercenaries, was not a new one. Feudal lords had long appreciated the value of using specially trained warrior bands to attack military targets ahead of the main force, or behind enemy lines. However, traditionally trained *samurai* questioned the ethics of this type of warfare. Moreover, the rate of attrition was high, so using well-trained and equipped military *ninja* formations became very costly.

The concept of mercenary *ninja* arose from simple beginnings. *Ronin* were leaderless warriors who

Ninja wore camouflage appropriate to the conditions under which an operation was mounted: here a night-time operation

had lost their lords and therefore their livelihood. Deprived of all status and property, they could not support themselves and since a descent into the contemptible peasant caste was unthinkable, suicide or banditry became the only alternatives. *Ronin* training enabled them to fight *samurai* on equal terms but they were not particularly effective at covert operations. Therefore, as one might expect, early *ninja* operations tended to be artless and often clumsy. However, as the Tokugawa Shogunate tightened its grip, a demand for more subtle mercenaries was created.

These formed around the earlier and successful operations, each adding to the core of training knowledge. Unsuccessful *ninja* and methods were ruthlessly weeded out by a process of natural selection. The *ninja* groups grew slowly until it was possible for them to stage small-scale group operations. However, the absence of proper military training resulted in a comparatively low standard of weapons proficiency and until the calibre of the orthodox fighting man had declined, later on into the shogunate, *samurai* generally defeated *ninja* in face-to-face engagements.

PRACTICE

Ninjutsu was a complete system of martial art, in many ways comparable to the more orthodox military traditions of feudal Japan. *Ninja* were proficient in a variety of martial activities, including archery, sword- and spear-work, throwing

weapons such as the star-wheel, camouflage, swimming, and un-armed combat. They were also skilled in concealing weapons. However, *ninja* operated by infiltration and stealth, rather than through the hand-to-hand encounters of regular warriors.

Ninja were trained to operate either as individuals, which required resourcefulness, patience and nerves of steel, or within groups, which required great co-ordination, dependability and thorough training. *Ninja* always used the least expected route to the victim. They trained to recognise the weak point, to go under, around, or over obstacles. Their senses were elevated to the point where the level of background noise provided clues to the whereabouts of opponents. Stillness coupled with camouflage rendered them virtually invisible.

The *ninja* were mercenaries – for hire to anyone and for any purpose – provided only that the price was right. In this second fundamental way, they differed from orthodox warriors who regarded their duty as sacred, and gave total loyalty to their lord, despising money. Since the typical *ninja* didn't come from warrior families, they would not be expected to hold military notions of honour.

Ninja services were hired through intermediaries. It was essential that the commissioning feudal lord, the *daimyo*, knew nothing overtly about the transaction, so he would not dishonour himself by lying under interrogation. Thus the *daimyo's* chief lieutenant – his *hatamoto* –

would learn of the lord's wishes that a particular enemy be removed, and he would then set the process in motion. Messages were left at particular shrines and contracts agreed between distant intermediaries, using the 'cell system' common to popular notions of espionage. If anyone was discovered, they could reveal only a small part of the undertaking.

The secret of success in *ninja* operations lay in the minute planning, which depended entirely on information. The *ninja* first needed knowledge of the victim's whereabouts, both the local geography and the disposition of fortifications, sentry posts and living quarters. The victim's location and habits could be learned through bribing servants, or by infiltrating *ninja* into the target's

The ninja sword was used to stab a victim for a silent kill. If the operation was discovered by vigilant sentries, the sword became the first line weapon in hand-to-hand combat

household as servants. There is an often reported tale of one *ninja* who hid in a privy until it was used by the intended victim. The *ninja* then fatally stabbed him with a spear.

When infiltration proved impossible, *ninja* observers reconnoitred target areas, sometimes for weeks on end, until they had a precise picture of the target household's operation and schedules. *Ninja* observers were trained to remain motionless for hours at a time and with careful camouflage it was possible to pass close to one and not see him.

Sometimes the victim was poisoned through his food or drink. Other times, he was attacked when he had little protection – such as during hunting. There is one reported instance where the lord was lured away from the main hunting party and brought near to a river running through otherwise open land. He felt reasonably secure because there appeared to be nowhere that danger could be concealed, but in fact a dozen *ninja* were submerged in the river, breathing through hollowed reeds. They emerged from the water, caught the horse and killed the victim.

Not all victims were killed by *ninja*; sometimes they were kidnapped and perhaps held to ransom. Under these circumstances, *ninja* had to subdue their victim and immobilise him without harming him. This made the operation doubly difficult in that *ninja* had not only to infiltrate into a household, but then leave noiselessly with a resisting captive.

WEAPONS AND EQUIPMENT

Because of their relative lack of combat effectiveness *ninja* were obliged to operate covertly. Special weapons which were developed included a sword, a short spear, strangling wires, throwing stars and caltrops. Samurai trained with standard weapons and their responses were geared to known tactics. Ninja weapons did not conform to the orthodox rules of engagement, so the *ninja* held an advantage. The sword was shorter than the normal *samurai* longsword and is usually shown with a square finger-guard, or *tsuba*. The shorter sword was more effective in confined spaces. The ninja spear was also shorter than the samurai's and it was commonly used in a jabbing action. Sometimes a short cord was attached to its haft, so it could be thrown a short distance and then retrieved.

Strangling wires were looped over the opponent's head, then the *ninja* quickly leaned forwards, dragging the unfortunate victim up and over his back. Body weight plus applied pressure ensured a quick kill. The knife, or *tanto*, was also extensively used as a close-range weapon and was usually driven upwards, below the angle of the victim's jaw, so it penetrated the brain, causing almost instantaneous death.

Throwing stars (*shuriken*) feature heavily in modern *ninja* films, though there is little historical evidence that they were in fact used widely. As their name implies, they consist of flat plates of star-shaped metal, with four or five sharp points. Sometimes the points were dipped in poison though this occasionally caused fatalities among *ninja* as they struggled to pull the stars free from their harnesses in the heat of battle. Throwing stars are slow weapons and rarely give a quick kill, so they tended not to be used in covert *ninja* operations.

For the same reasons bows also tended to be used in the overt part of an engagement, covering the retreat of the infiltrators with a murderous cross-fire. Caltrops are metal spikes, so made that sharp points project upwards and into the feet of unwary pursuers. They were scattered by retreating *ninja* to slow pursuit.

▼ and ▶ *Ninja believed that they could harness the body's natural powers by means of 'Nine Ways Cutting'. This took the form of meditation using various hand symbols according to the power they wished to draw on*

Ninja are also said to have used primitive cannon fashioned from hollowed bamboo canes bound with rope. Needless to say, such contraptions cannot have withstood a high breech pressure and either had an ineffective range, or blew the *ninja* up! More effective were smoke bombs which acted as primitive forms of tear-gas to distract pursuers. Some of these were thrown by means of a slingshot. Gunpowder charges were used to burst open gates and bring down the roof on the heads of attacking soldiers.

Ninja reached their target by a variety of means, the most usual being to scale walls using cloth-covered grapples, three-barbed hooks attached to a length of light rope. They were thrown upwards against the wall, and lodged in drain channels and chinks in masonry. *Ninja* were trained to worm their way through narrow windows and arrow slits, falling safely from heights and landing on all fours, as a cat does. It is claimed that they were even able to walk silently across what were called 'nightingale floors', wooden floors made deliberately so that they creaked noisily when walked on.

Individual *ninja* swam across slow-flowing rivers except when their wet clothes would either give them away, or provide a trail for pursuers to follow. In such cases they used boats, or an ingenious if cumbersome arrangement of baskets on their feet, in which they poled across the river. Although this tactic is well reported in *ninja* chronicles, there is little evidence to suggest that it was often used.

Horses were used by the nobility, so a *ninja* on horseback would have attracted a great deal of attention. Instead, *ninja* were trained for endurance and could cover a great deal of ground on foot.

MYSTICAL *NINJA*

Kuji kiri or 'nine ways cutting', is part of the mystical tradition of ninjutsu. *Ninja* believed that the body's natural powers could be focused toward off a sword cut, or to make the *ninja* invisible. Certainly the well-camouflaged *ninja* was extremely difficult to see and such claims reinforced the *ninja*'s image as an invincible warrior. There is also some evidence to suggest that *kuji kiri* strengthened the *ninja*'s self-confidence and quietened fear.

Samurai claimed that *ninja* were in league with demons, and that *kuji kiri* represented one of the ways that demonic power was harnessed.

Kuji kiri was invoked through meditation, the *ninja*'s attention turned inwards, banishing fear and apprehension, and replacing it with a calm and purposeful mind. The fingers of the hands lace together in one or more of nine different ways, according to the specific power which the *ninja* wished to invoke.

Many *ninja* were Buddhists of the Tendai sect and when about to die, uttered the words '*Namu Amida Butsu!*', or 'In the name of Buddha Amitabha'.

Buddha is the embodiment of pity and compassion and calling on his name was believed to ensure that their souls would be transported to heaven. Certainly *ninja* could expect no mercy when caught alive.

PRESENT-DAY NINJUTSU

Despite a few claims to the contrary, ninjutsu died out many years ago. However, a revival of interest in it has stimulated some Japanese business people to create a *ninja* training camp in the foothills of Mount Fuji. This is offered in the same spirit as American Wild West Towns that stage mock gunfights.

The camp is laid out as a traditional Japanese village with a row of modern houses set out in thickly wooded land. The houses are far from standard and contain secret rooms, hidden tunnels and concealed places for ambush. Would-be *ninja* are shown how to cross streams with water-shoes, climb steep walls with grappling irons and stalk silently. *Ninja* games include sprinting from one firing point to another, loosing off three darts from a blowgun, throwing a couple of stars into a man-sized target and then racing off to the next point.

Though this is obviously not a serious study, other activities of the Nippon Ninja Society are. For example, much useful material has arisen through the society's programme of interviewing descendants of known *ninja* families. All reliable sources of information support the view that ninjutsu has now died out and no vestiges of traditional practice remain.

SHORINJI KEMPO

HISTORY

Shorinji kempo is the Japanese rendering of the Chinese Shaolin su chuan'fa, the martial art system of the Shaolin Monastery from where legend has it most modern martial arts originated. Several organisations in Japan during the early-mid 20th century claimed a connection to the monastery but the one which has been most successful in this is the Shorinji Kempo founded by the late Doshin So.

DOSHIN SO

Doshin So was born Nakano Michiomi in 1911, the eldest son of

a customs officer in Okayama Prefecture, Japan. His father died when he was young, and he went to live with his grandfather in Manchuria. At this time Japan had invaded China and established military control. Both So's father and grandfather had been members of an ultra-nationalistic right-wing Japanese political party known as 'the Black Dragon Society'. So returned to Japan when his grandfather died and enrolled with the society.

He returned to Manchuria in 1928 to spy for the government, and began practising Chinese martial art under a Taoist priest. He travelled extensively through China and came eventually to Beijing, where he trained under Master Wen Lou shi in the *i-he chuan*. He also visited the Shaolin Monastery at Sungshan and was impressed by the famous scroll showing monks of different nationalities training together in martial art.

Some historians doubt that the highly secretive Chinese would teach their techniques without a long period of apprenticeship, even assuming that So could have convinced them that he was Chinese. It is highly unlikely that any master worth his salt would have taught foreigners, especially one of the Japanese overlords. Nevertheless, So's Nippon Shorinji Kempo has indisputable links with the Shaolin monastery, though the precise nature of these links is unclear.

So escaped from Manchuria ahead of the invading Russian forces, and returned in 1945 to a war-ravaged Japan. He began train-

◄ Nippon shorinji kempo is a Japanese attempt to re-create the martial art of the Shaolin Temple

▼ Students train in pairs using both striking and grappling techniques

▼ Exponents of Shorinji kempo wear lightweight white training tunics, with a dark over-hassock. The belt is thick and tubular, and unlike that used in other martial arts

SHORINJI KEMPO THEN AND NOW

Shorinji kempo is a comprehensive fighting system developed by its Japanese founder, Doshin So. So claimed that its techniques were based on those of the Shaolin Temple (hence Shorin ji kempo, the Japanese reading of Shaolin su chuan'fa) but connections between the two are hard to make. Impact techniques are collected into that part of the syllabus known as goho. Grappling techniques are collected under juho. Advanced training uses a pre-arranged routine of both elements in what is known as the embu.

ing in the *hakko ryu* school of jiu jitsu, a style founded in 1938 by Okuyama Yoshiharu and a branch development from the famous *daito ryu aikijiu jitsu*, taught to Okuyama by Master Matsuda Hosaku. After mastering it, he left the *hakko ryu* and founded the *Nippon Densei-to Shorinji Kempo* but court action by other shorinji kempo schools obliged him to change the name to the *Nippon Shorinji Kempo*. The tradition he founded has grown and the title of Grandmaster has now passed to his daughter. The association's headquarters are on the Japanese island of Chikoku.

TECHNIQUES

The martial art of the Shaolin temple was mainly concerned with weapon training, yet no weapons are used in shorinji kempo. Shorinji kempo grappling techniques are extremely sophisticated, and are far in advance of Chinese methods. They are, in fact, identical to jiu jitsu

The embu *is a polished performance of several techniques and responses. Performed by a pair of experts, the* embu *is virtually indistinguishable from free sparring*

techniques. Shorinji kempo striking techniques use hip action in a way not usually found with shaolin methods, though the fist is certainly used in the same way – there is no twist of the forearm on impact, such as in karate.

In many ways, the practical side of training is less important than the spiritual, for shorinji kempo enshrines the religio-philosophical concept of *kongo zen*, or having a mind like a diamond. This philosophy was originated in the years after the Second World War, when the Japanese economy was crippled and its administration was being supervised by the Americans. So was concerned at the decline of the Japanese people's morale and proposed *kongo zen* as a self-help philosophy.

Kongo zen teaches that everything comes from within. So's followers do not believe in any form of godhead, but are concerned only with achieving an understanding of life. By means of meditation, the mind learns to let go of the emotions which cloud its otherwise clear perception. When anger, aggression, fear and desire have gone, what remains is an unclouded intelligence, capable of acting swiftly and without emotion. This is why each lesson includes a period of seated meditation, or *za zen*. The class sits cross-legged in straight lines and consciousness is focused inwards. A senior student moves around the class, using a staff as a straight-edge to test and correct each student's posture. Meditation is brought to a stop when the senior

1 *Shorinji kempo striking techniques are fast and flowing, using precise application of carefully targeted strikes, rather than sledgehammer*

blows. Here, an attack is begun with a long reverse punch to the head. The partner shifts his weight over the rear foot and blocks

2 *The reverse punch has shifted weight off the rear foot and this is then lifted quickly into a roundhouse kick*

student bangs the staff against the floor.

The practical techniques of shorinji kempo can be divided broadly into two parts, *goho* and *juho*. *Goho* techniques are generally the first to be performed in the training session. They consist of striking techniques such as the punch. This is performed with a long-hand action and the fist does not rotate on impact but remains thumb-upwards. Kicks are performed with a snapping action, rather than with a straight thrust. Front kick, round-house kick and side kick are all performed. These basic techniques (*kihon*) are performed in conjunction with body movements and blocks. The training is typically Japanese, with students all performing the same techniques in formal class lines. Basic practice may also be practised with a partner. Senior grades partner lower grades and in this way, the senior comes to learn more about the technique through explaining it, and the junior grade benefits from the individual tuition.

Higher grades are taught *atemi waza*, the techniques of attacking the opponent's vital points. Some of these attacks are said to be lethal, while others cause unconsciousness or paralysis. These same vital points are used in a form of massage known as *seiho*, which stimulates the flow of energy through the body and is said to improve health.

Juho techniques use the principles of yielding to the attacker's strength, harmonising with his movement and then re-directing it. There are some 300 *juho* techniques

which include wrist, elbow and shoulder locks, and a variety of throws. Typically the attack is deflected and the opponent diverted with a strike to a weak point. A lock or throw is then employed.

Once a student is proficient in *juho* techniques he begins to practise a form of pre-arranged sparring known as an *embu*, or performance. This combines *juho* and *goho* techniques into a flowing sequence,

In this sequence, the attacker's punch is blocked and there is a simultaneous punch direct to his solar plexus

The punch is sharply withdrawn, the energy for this being used to help power a thrust with palm-heel to the side of the opponent's jaw

which is indistinguishable from the free sparring of experts.

Kata are also performed and may be either solitary or pair form. A series of combination techniques linking attack with defence form the foundation of each kata. Coloured belt grades must learn a total of eight kata, each one performed to a count. Free sparring makes use of either *juho* or *goho* techniques but the two are never mixed. Competitions are sometimes held, though winning is played down in favour of participation for its own sake.

There are five grades in the shorinji kempo syllabus, with a six-month interval between them. Each grade is identified by a coloured belt:

5th grade	white belt
4th grade	yellow belt
3rd grade	green belt
2nd grade	blue belt
1st grade	brown belt

The interval between brown and black belt is a year, which is spent revising the entire syllabus. Before taking the black belt examination each student is required to take three oaths: the pledge or *seiku*, a holy maxim (*seigan*) and the creed, or *shinjo*. Once a student has become a black belt he is entitled to wear a black over-tunic and tubular belt. Senior grades are admitted into the association as monks, though unlike the classical Buddhist monk, they are allowed to marry.

SILAT

Silat, or more correctly pentjak silat, is an Indonesian martial art built around Islam. It has both armed and unarmed forms, the latter using strikes, punches and kicks. The art's origins are unknown, though it seems to have drawn on Thai and Chinese sources for its techniques. Judo and karate techniques have also been incorporated in the last 50 years. Some schools of silat have developed rules for competition but others consider that this will destroy the system's fighting effectiveness. The numerous islands of Indonesia have developed equally numerous styles. Local variations have sprung up around particular masters, or guru, and a lack of interchange between schools has perpetuated these divisions.

Silat is often practised to music, as Thai boxing is, which has led to a common misunderstanding that it involves elements of dance.

The first obstacle is finding a guru who will take you, which is often difficult as the best masters have no shortage of applicants and can afford to be choosy. Successful candidates swear an oath on the Koran and begin their training during the late evenings. Arduous day-time training is made difficult by the heat and humidity. Training is usually performed by lamplight, and the novice is first introduced to the element of ritual. Next he learns how to form the various body weapons. These are used to attack specific areas of the body, such that knife-hand is used against the ribs, knuckles are driven into the temples and elbows are used to attack the opponent's ribs.

Posture teaches the student how to be effective in any position, for it is not always possible to position yourself carefully before responding to an attack. Sparring exercises involve single and multiple partners. More advanced students learn about the body's vital points, and how to attack them. Weapons training, taught only to advanced students, teaches the use of the sword, knife, staff, stick, and unusual weapons such as the chain and forked truncheon, which is similar to the Okinawan *sai* and is used in the same manner. Most senior students are pitted against a number of armed opponents.

Curiously, spiritual training is taught last of all. Its objective is to help the student to pass beyond physical technique, so his practice becomes an art form.

Some forms of silat are taught secretly. The public see them only in remarkable demonstrations in which the practitioners lapse into trances and appear to be impervious to sword thrusts.

Bersilat is a Malaysian martial art closely related to silat. It has undergone a drift in technique so that nowadays it is largely practised as a dance form, using movements and techniques which, though based on martial art technique, are no longer effective in that respect. There are a number of schools practising an effective form of bersilat though they are not open to the public.

SUMO

HISTORY

The name sumo derives from the Japanese word *sumai*, meaning struggle. It is one of the oldest forms of combat, and its most distant ancestor is the hand-to-hand fighting of primeval man, before even the advent of weapons. Pushing and shoving are the earliest forms of fighting, and later these evolve into punching and kicking. Much later on, techniques using leverage are introduced. Sumo was born from this common process and the first recorded match is described in the famous *Nihon Shoki* chronicles of AD 720.

Legend has it that in 23 BC Emperor Suinjin witnessed a match between Tajima noh-Kehaya and Nomi noh-Sukune. Sukune drove Kehaya to the ground with a kick and then stamped on him, causing

injuries from which he died. Sumo was therefore very much a brutal, anything-goes type of engagement, the object of which was either to force an opponent to give in, or to kill him.

Though a true fighting art, sumo as such did not initially form a part of the warrior's training. Virtually all military engagement entailed weapons, and unarmed combat

occupied only an insignificant part of the martial syllabus. Nevertheless, many warriors did study methods of striking and kicking to ward off opponents who got close. Grappling too was studied, with the object of restraining opponents, or of taking them prisoner. Many of these techniques were taken from sumo and, in particular, the thrusting kicks which owe so much to body action.

Sumo became popular and eventually rudimentary rules were introduced to limit the lethal techniques. The object of a match changed to defeating an opponent without killing him. Royal patronage during the

Nara period (710-794) resulted in the adoption of courtesy-ritual, and an annual competition was established. Skilled wrestlers (*sumotori*) had a privileged social status and favoured performers were retained by the court. This changed during the Heian period of 794-1185, when once more sumo's combat effectiveness was stressed.

Warriors indulged in wrestling as part of their fitness training and during the Kamakura period (1185-1333), sumo was widely practised in an adapted form called *kumi-uchi*. Sumo continued to develop in the ensuing Muromachi and Momoyama periods too, but the introduction of firearms began to change the face of warfare, and group engagements replaced the classical individual combat. When warfare died down during the Tokugawa Shogunate emphasis was once more shifted to the sporting aspect. During the Edo period of 1600-

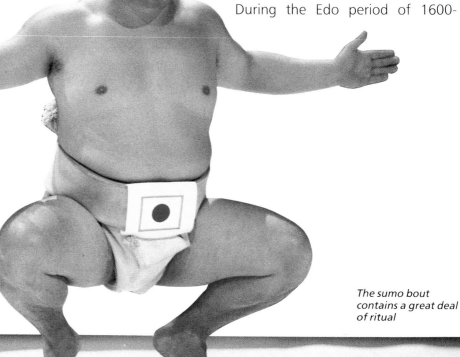

The sumo bout contains a great deal of ritual

◀ The wrestlers scatter
salt as part of the
preliminaries to a
bout

▼ They crouch down
and face each other

also arrange their hair in a special manner known as the *ichomage*.

The wrestlers all eat together from an iron cauldron containing *chanko nabe*, a stew made from either fish or meat and vegetables such as cabbage, onions and spinach. Tofu increases the protein content, and a rich stock with soy sauce gives flavour. Each wrestler is expected to consume several bowls, together with rice. This is washed down with liberal supplies of beer.

COMPETITIONS

Wrestlers are escorted to the competition area by a sword bearer (*tachimochi*) and an attendant (*tsuyuhari*).

An elaborate ritual precedes the match proper, with both wrestlers throwing handfuls of salt into the air. They take up wide straddle stances and face each other, knuckles resting on the floor. Even

1868 sumo's popularity increased enormously, to a level which has been sustained to the present day.

PRESENT-DAY PRACTICE

Grand champions are allowed to wear an embroidered apron, or *kessho-mewashi*, a tradition which originates from the 17th century when the *sumotori* Akashi became embarrassed by his nudity and wrapped a standard around himself before his presentation to the emperor. Grand champions may

139

The loser is the wrestler who touches the floor with any part of his body except the soles of his feet

then the match does not start, for this setting up occurs twice before they rise simultaneously against one another.

The sumo bout is determined when one wrestler forces another out of the ring, or makes him touch the ground with any part of his body other than the soles of his feet. Leverage is applied by grasping a thick band, worn around the waist and dipping between the legs to protect the groin. Slapping techniques and pushing are allowed, but attacks below the waist are not.

The form of competition favours the heavy man. Although ability and martial art spirit are major factors, ultimately weight cannot be ignored and a lighter wrestler is simply bulldozed from the ring by a less skilled but much heavier opponent.

TRAINING

Training routines use the *shiko*, or lifting each leg to the side as high as possible and then thumping it back down again. The palms are pressed against the knees and the body hunches forward. The wrestler squats to the floor and extends each leg alternately out to the side. Then he sinks down to a sitting position and spreads his legs as wide as possible. He leans forward as far as his great girth will allow him in the exercise known as *matawari*. The *teppo* or 'iron cannon' is a solid baulk of timber against which the *sumotori* pushes. Both hands are used, or each alternately in a series of full bodyweight palm-heels.

APPRENTICESHIP AND GRADING

New wrestlers are admitted through a form of apprenticeship. Intake is related to the six annual tournaments and is supervised by a board of senior officials. Prospective apprentices must be heavy enough to pass the weigh-in. If they succeed they join a club in which they are taught the basic techniques of sumo and the rituals of practice. Each prospective wrestler may take a fighting name, or *shikona*.

Sumotori are arranged by grade according to their ability, and the more accomplished wrestler is deferred to by less skilled colleagues. Recruits are known as *maezumo* and when they have trained in the basic techniques they rank as *honchu*, or beginner. They begin their wrestling career in sumo's third rank, at the first stage, or *jo nokuchi*. From there they rise successively to the *jo nidan* and the *sandanme*. At this point they cross over into the second rank at the grade of *makushita*. After a number of successful bouts they become contenders (*ju ryo*) for admission to the first rank. The first rank (*maku uchi*) of *sumotori* contains senior wrestlers (*maegashira*) from which are drawn the pre-champions, or *komusubi*, the junior champions (*sekiwake*) and the champions – the *ozeki*. From the most successful of the champions are drawn the grand champions, or *yokozuna*.

All movement between these ranks is based on performance at the annual tournaments.

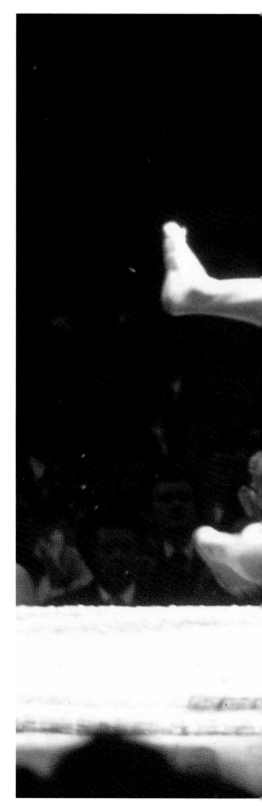

TRAINING AND TACTICS

If ever there was a correct size and shape for a martial art, sumo defines it! If you are very, very stout and heavy, you have the right build to succeed. The lower your centre of gravity, the more difficult it is for an opponent to lever you over and the heavier you are, the more you can withstand his strength. Yet despite his great bulk, the sumo wrestler must be able to move explosively and be tough enough to withstand powerful impacts.

TAEKWONDO

The name taekwondo means 'way of the foot and fist'.

HISTORY

Taekwondo has evolved out of a number of separate sources, though the name itself was first used in 1953. Korea developed its own sophisticated martial art traditions but the Japanese occupation of Korea between 1907 and 1945 led to a suppression of all Korean martial art practices and eventually to their replacement with Japanese martial art ways. However, the old martial arts were not completely eradicated and traces insinuated their way into the training.

Actually, Korean martial arts involve two highly characteristic activities, both of which clearly distinguish them from all forms of Japanese systems. The first is the high, circling kicks and the second is the employment of destruction tests to measure the power produced in a strike. The high kicks were probably introduced from northern shaolin kung fu schools. Contrast this with the low kicks imported by Okinawan *karateka* from the southern shaolin systems. Karate copied many Korean circling kicks in the late 1950s and early 1960s.

◄ *Modern taekwondo has developed out of several different and earlier sources*

Taekwondo is noted for its high kicks and for its emphasis on destruction techniques

Breaking techniques are derived from the hard shaolin schools, where they are used to test the conditioning of the hands and arms. Just as muscles are trained to operate efficiently over long periods, so the body weapons are trained so they can deliver tremendous impacts without being damaged. This requires a conditioning process, so the skin thickens and becomes less prone to laceration, and bone produces reinforcing callus. Curiously, destruction testing has survived in taekwondo but the conditioning process seems to have been lost.

High kicks and breaking techniques are common to all three of the present Korean martial arts.

Taekwondo was the name given to all the Korean martial arts. It was an umbrella title, introduced by the government to include tang soo do and hapkido. This was not well received and its imposition provoked large-scale defections, so many of Korea's major martial arts schools were divided. Those which merged under taekwondo's umbrella have standardised their syllabus and performance, so the original differences between the styles are now all but submerged. The unified taekwondo syllabus has developed a long way and taekwondo is now recognised by the International Olympic Committee.

TECHNIQUES

There are many similarities between the practice of taekwondo and karate, not just as a result of their previous close association but also because there are only a limited number of ways in which the hands and feet can be used as weapons. The jumping kicks are, however, quite distinct.

Jumping kicks

Jumping kicks are made with an explosive muscular action of the legs, driving the body high into the air and thrusting the foot hard into the target with the other foot also clear of the floor. The hip joints must be flexible because the leg moves through a wide range and agility is essential because the kick must be performed without run-up or early warning. You must know firstly where your opponent is, and secondly where you are relative to him. This is easy when you have both feet firmly on the floor but it is more difficult when he is moving

Jumping kick
1 *Begin from a high stance*

2 *Bring your rear foot forward and up, as though you were going to stand on an imaginary chair*

1

2

and you are both leaping and spinning around at the same time!

Jumping front kick and a version of jumping roundhouse kick both use the ball of the foot, whereas the other version uses the instep. Jumping side kick uses the heel/edge of the foot and jumping back kick strikes home with the heel; jumping reverse roundhouse kick uses either the heel or the sole of the foot and jumping circling kicks use the inside and outside edges of the feet.

Front kick Begin from a high stance with knees slightly flexed. Jump high into the air and depending on the range, rise vertically upwards, or diagonally towards your opponent. The more vertically you jump, the higher the kick will be. Kick before you reach maximum height, raising both knees and snap kicking with the ball of your foot to your opponent's upper chest or face.

Improve the style of your kick by lifting the supporting leg well clear of the floor as you kick and by keeping your elbows to your sides; many novices flap their arms as they jump. Land on the balls of your feet with both knees slightly bent. Quickly take up an effective guard, so you can ward off a fast counter-attack.

Double front kick A jumping double front kick is very like a jumping front kick except that both feet strike home, one after the other. Begin as for the previous example, first raising your left knee and snap kicking, then snap kicking

3 *Kick before your jump reaches maximum height, tucking up the trailing leg*

▼ **Double front kick**
1 *Kick with your left leg as you jump*

2 *Then kick with your right foot as you are still rising*

▼ **Roundhouse kick**
▼ **1** *Jump up and turn your hip so the kicking leg leads*

2 *Lash out with the kicking leg as you are turning in mid-air*

with the right leg while you are still in flight. Deliver the first kick as you are rising, and the action will pull your body still higher for the second kick. Keep your arms to your sides, land poised and take up an effective guard.

Roundhouse kick Jumping roundhouse kick starts in exactly the same way as the previous pair of examples. As you are rising, first twist your shoulders, then turn your hips in the direction that the kick will travel. This spins your body and your foot can snap out horizontally into the target. Withdraw your kicking knee to your body and land poised, on the balls of your feet.

TRAINING AND TACTICS

Jumping kicks rely on plyometric strength in the legs, so train for this first. Regardless of the kick to be practised, it is essential that you begin the kicking action even as your body is rising. The developing kick serves to lift your body even higher. Jumping/turning kicks need good spatial awareness, so you can keep track of where you are in relation to your opponent.

1 Side kick
Spin around in the air and thrust out your kicking foot. Pull the trailing leg up and maintain an effective guard

2 Back kick
Jump away from the opponent, turning your back as you do so. Thrust out the kicking leg with heel leading

3 Reverse roundhouse kick
This uses a full 360° spin in the air, the kicking leg extending even before the hips turn fully into the target

Side kick Jumping side kick begins in the same way, except that both knees are pulled to the chest. Twist around as you rise, so one hip turns towards your opponent. As you turn, thrust out the kicking foot, which will drag your body fully sideways-on. Pull your foot into a side kick position, so the heel and outer edge lead. Tuck the non-kicking leg up. Gather the spent kick back in, and land on the balls of your feet. Alternatively, kick by springing diagonally up from a back stance, twisting in the air as you do so.

Back kick Jumping kick is generally performed from a vertical spring, or from a jump away from the opponent. Jump high and begin turning your body away from the target. Don't wait until you turn fully before thrusting out a back kick. The kicking action draws your body into the correct configuration.

Reverse roundhouse kick Jumping reverse roundhouse kick uses a spring and a 360-degree turn of the body. Lift both knees to your chest and spin around in the air. As with the previous kick, don't wait until you turn fully before performing the kick itself. Make sure that your heel leads into the target.

BREAKING TECHNIQUES

No-one under 18 should practise these techniques, which can damage young knuckle and toe joints, possibly deforming them permanently.

TRAINING AND TACTICS

Jumping side kick, back kick and reverse roundhouse kick are the most difficult to perform. You must be able to visualise your opponent's position at all times.

kick it! The target area is too small and a miss may cause injury.

Performance The first thing to try and break is a single, planed pitch pine board. This should be perfectly dry, and measure not less than 30 by 20 cm by 25 mm (12 × 8 × 1 inch) thick. Provided it is dry it will certainly break with only a very small impact. However, do be aware that parana pine is quite hard and even a single piece may require a substantial impact.

No matter how powerful the strike, the board will only break if it is held stiffly. Experts can break unsupported boards but their activities lie outside the scope of this advice. Use two colleagues to hold the board, so its major axis is vertical. Both stand in forward stances, with their leading knees close together and back legs locked out straight. The board is held with a palm-heel grip, the fingers being tucked carefully away from injury. Both pairs of supporting arms are locked straight.

Test the rigidity of the grip by pushing against the board and get your partners to adjust their position until the board is set at exactly the correct angle and height. Begin from a left fighting stance and punch right through the board. Don't try to focus actually on the board and don't twist your fist on impact. Make a loud shout on impact. If the board doesn't break, find out why before trying a second time. It may be damp, in which case continued efforts will only damage your knuckles.

CONDITIONING

The ball of your foot is already quite toughened by training in bare feet but your knuckles are not and should be conditioned if you want to practise breaking techniques.

Form your fist correctly by using a punching post. This is best padded with slick, hard rubber, so it can be cleaned after use. Stand in a fighting stance close to the post with your left leg and arm leading. Withdraw your leading arm and lean behind a punch into the post. Do not twist your fist on impact! The punch begins and ends with the knuckles uppermost. Do not use full power but gradually increase intensity through the session. Repeated pounding on the post will help you roll your fingers tightly into the palm, so they don't bark against the target. It also teaches you how to align your wrist, so power can flow in a straight line.

Use the punching post also for knife, ridge hand, and any other hand techniques – but don't try to

◄ *A fast and hard kick can break a dry pine board even when it is poorly supported*

▼ *There are two types of competition: one uses padded waistcoats and headguards, the other fist mitts and padded boots*

them immediately. Use only the unfinished house brick of the type known as a 'flitten'.

Breeze blocks are made from compressed ash. Though anything up to 12 cm/4½ inches thick, they are not hard to break – provided always that they are well supported at either end. Place the supporting bricks as close to the end of the block as possible, because this allows for maximum leverage and an easier break.

Ice is hard, but it is also extremely brittle. A huge block can be shattered with one blow, providing that it is long enough in relation to its width and thickness. Once the block is smashed, leave your hand among the shards for a second or so to melt any razor edges near your wrists!

COMPETITION

Taekwondo competitions are held on a taped 8-metre square. Four corner judges score your performance, writing down their awards on

A front kick break uses the ball of the foot. The board is held so its minor axis is vertical. This allows it to break to either side of your foot, rather than closing like jaws on your ankle! The height of the board must be lowered and it should be angled so the kick meets it at right angles. Any other position and the foot may skate painfully off it.

Do not attempt to break wood with either the tips of your fingers or your instep: both require considerable pre-training and even a thin board will injure otherwise untoughened body parts. Do not break wood with a head butt! Although spectacular, it produces spectacular brain damage!

When you can break one board, move up to two. It is even more essential that these are anchored firmly. Also, if you are using perfectly square sections of board, do make sure that both pieces have the grain running in the same direction.

Boards always break along the grain. Having said that, boards of the right type are very expensive so many experienced taekwondo practitioners now use chipboard. This has no grain and breaks occur because of the brittle adhesive used to hold the wood chips together.

Roofing tiles and bricks can also be broken. Tiles must first be covered with a handkerchief because they break into dagger-like shards. Build a stack of them supported on two concrete blocks and if you want to make it easier, separate each tile with pieces of wooden packing. The first tile breaks the one below it, and so on.

Oven-dry bricks are easy to break but once they have absorbed moisture from the air, they become all but unbreakable. If you are not sure whether they are suitable for breaking, put them in the oven on a low heat setting for several hours. Let them cool in the oven, and then use

Full-power kicks to the head are permitted and a knockout by this means determines the outcome of a bout

score forms which are collected by the referee at the end of the bout and passed to the jury of two senior refereeing officials.

Dress and protective equipment

You must wear clean and unripped training tunics, over which an approved padded jacket is worn. One jacket is red, the other blue to distinguish the two contestants for scoring. Groin guards and head guards must be used. Spectacles are not allowed, and neither may you wear training shoes. Jewellery must be removed. You may wear bandages if they relate to injuries sustained in the present competition, otherwise they are not allowed.

Weight categories

Competitions involve individual bouts held in weight categories.

Timing

Each match is of three three-minute bouts, with a minute's rest between each, though these times can be varied by the event organiser in response to the schedule. Match time is halted when the referee calls the doctor.

Scoring

The outcome of the match is decided by a knockout by a legitimate technique. Failing this, you can win by amassing more point scores than your opponent. Scores are awarded for technically skilful techniques which land on the scoring areas of the head and body. Head kicks are regarded as more difficult than punches and in a tied bout the contestant who performed the most valid head kicks may well win.

Penalties

The referee can disqualify contestants for intentional fouls. For less serious infractions, the referee calls the contestants to their standing positions and imposes a one-point penalty on the offender. Half-point penalties are imposed for less serious infractions.

All protests must be made in writing and submitted to the board of arbitration appointed for that purpose by the tournament organisers.

TAIHO JUTSU

HISTORY

Originally the *samurai* enforced the laws passed by the lord of a Japanese feudal fief. They therefore functioned both as police force and as warriors, protecting the fief against aggression both from without and within. As the feudal system weakened in favour of more centralised control, it became necessary to create a national police force capable of controlling an increasingly rowdy section of the populace in Japan's ever-growing cities.

There were three types of early police – the *metsuke* or secret police, a well-trained anti-insurgency force with its membership taken from the ranks of the military; the *meikashi* and the *okapiki*, policing the rural and metropolitan areas respectively.

Peace during the Tokugawa Shogunate led to an increase in population. Furthermore, increasing use of conscript soldiers meant that weapons – once the exclusive possession of the *samurai* – became available to a larger segment of the population. Faced with escalating rowdiness and violence, the police developed a system called *yaku kobujutsu* (martial art techniques for officials). This included five parts, the first being *bojutsu*, or staff techniques. The modern name for *yaku kobujutsu* is *taiho jutsu*.

TECHNIQUES

The *bo* was almost 2 metres/6 feet long and was usually made from a dense, smooth Japanese wood similar to oak. Its size made it possible to fight from a stand-off position, using wide swings to knock the opponent's feet away, or short jabs to his solar plexus. The *bo* could even break a sword by means of a hard strike to the flat of the blade and was so tough it could withstand all but a direct sword-cut. Its smooth finish made it difficult for the opponent to seize hold. However, its sheer size and weight were handicaps. It needed a lot of space to be deployed properly, and a lot of upper body strength to move it quickly.

Hanbo jutsu used a shorter staff, allowing faster deployment in a more confined area. The *hanbo* has survived to the present day and is used by Tokyo riot police – a lasting commendation to its value as a police weapon. The *hanbo* can trap an opponent and in the hands of a skilled user provides a good defence against a sword. It is effective in stunning and can be used to lock the elbow and shoulder joints.

The *jutte* was a metal truncheon with a tine protruding from and parallel to the baton. Some types had a pointed end which with a little practice could be thrown through a criminal's foot, pinning it to the ground. Used the other way around the *jutte* made an effective stun. The tine gave the fingers some protection and under certain circumstances, it could even trap the blade of a sword. *Jutte* were sometimes used in pairs, forming x-blocks to ward off weapon attacks, and jabbing with the butt ends to wind or stun the opponent.

The traditional way for dealing with a swordsman involved three long-handled weapons – the forked *sasumata* to catch the sword-wielding arm, the barbed *sodegarami* for tangling his clothes and preventing him from withdrawing, and the t-shaped *tsukubo* which prevented him from rushing in and hacking at the policemen.

Hojo jutsu was the technique of tying, by which a resisting suspect could be bound. Different methods were prescribed for tying men and women and a one-handed system was developed. This allowed the free hand to restrain the suspect as his limbs were being pinioned. *Hojo jutsu* was extracted from the classical warrior's training, where it was used to capture victims for ransom or interrogation.

The police also needed to grapple with a criminal, inflicting enough pain to subdue him, but not so much that he was damaged. The official police grappling system was known as *kogusoku* and its syllabus included painful joint locks, immobilising holds and throws.

MODERN ARREST TECHNIQUES

Any martial art can provide the basis for a police arrest system. However, certain arts are more adaptable than others: for example, the striking-based arts are socially unsuitable for police use, whereas the old Japanese methods of grappling are appropriate. These apply leverage to the joints, permitting a controlled

Striking-based martial arts are unsuitable for police use. The emphasis is on controlling the miscreant, not flattening him!

degree of force to be applied. Only the mildest forms of diversionary strikes may be used.

Selecting the appropriate starting point is not as easy as one might imagine. Many modern martial arts are thought to be effective means of self-defence, but in fact have become too stylised, or altered for sporting purposes to be truly effective. Demonstrations involve unrealistic attacks. The knife is held obligingly out for the arm to be grabbed; the attacker swings a punch and then freezes as the counter-attack is made; and so on. To determine whether a system is effective as self defence it needs to be tested realistically and frequently. The system must be teachable within a limited time and it must have a wide application.

The police have selected a mixed aikido- and judo-based system. One of its most obvious characteristics is that it operates on the move. The attacker's force is taken and extended, so he loses the initiative. The system uses restraining locks which immobilise the wrist, elbow and shoulder joints. Simple judo throws and groundwork are taught. The police have noted that many scuffles result in both parties falling to the floor. The groundwork system is aimed not at teaching the officer to perform sophisticated hold-downs but at getting him to think in a prone position.

Some martial art critics have felt the groundwork techniques could be a little more effective, although to get them to the stage where they could be used in actual arrests

TRAINING AND TACTICS

Self-defence techniques must be performed on the move. Your opponent won't stand idly by as you twist various parts of his anatomy, so be prepared to move with him. Techniques must allow a wide latitude on the part of your opponent. It is no use pinning your hopes on one which requires your opponent to behave precisely as you want him to.

would take too long. Senior martial artists tended to promote techniques to be used in arrests which, though effective when performed by them, were too advanced for unskilled police officers.

As it is, the police self-defence system is a masterpiece of organisation, using a series of interlocking techniques. All superfluous techniques have been pruned away and what remains is capable of wide application despite a short period of training.

Not all police arrest techniques are unarmed. There is also a need for the officer to use his truncheon effectively. Longer staffs are coming into use for controlling more serious outbreaks of violence. Both weapons must be fitted into a

1 Jab the assailant in the chest with your staff . . .

2 . . . then insert the staff under his arm

3 Step around and apply an arm-entangle, using the staff to provide leverage

simply steps back, lowering his body at the same time, which forces the attacker down to his knees.

The second example uses the staff to block an incoming grab, knocking it upwards and over the head. Then it is brought around sharply, rapping the attacker across his elbow, or on the side of his knee. The staff is slid under his other arm as the officer steps around to the side. The attacker's arm is trapped around the staff and the officer presses down with his leading hand while levering up with the rear hand. This applies pressure to the shoulder joint and forces the attacker to the floor. The staff's length supplies considerable leverage, so only a minimum amount of effort is needed to achieve control.

scheme and the following pair of examples indicates the refined simplicity of what has been devised.

In the first example, the attacker attempts to push the police officer in the chest. The officer draws his truncheon and brings it around the back of the attacker's wrist. He takes hold of the other end and traps the attacker's hand, then

TANG SOO DO

HISTORY

The earliest indications of military activity in the Korean peninsula appear in the wall paintings of tombs constructed during the Kokuryo Dynasty (AD 37-668), which show men dressed in loincloths and using what appears to be unarmed combat to defeat opponents. Apart from this, there is no early conclusive historical record.

An elite warrior caste emerged in the south-eastern kingdom of divided Korea and during the Silla Dynasty (AD 668-935), expanded beyond and with Chinese military support, over-ran the neighbouring kingdom of Baekje. The conquering Korean military elite was known as the *hwa rang*, or 'way of flowering youth'. These warriors were accomplished horsemen, archers and swordsmen. It is claimed that they were also adept at unarmed combat but in all one-to-one armed engagements, this has a lower priority than proficiency with weapons.

The *hwa rang* operated a code of behaviour akin to the chivalry of European medieval knights. This was known as *hwarang-do*, though nowadays the same term is misused to describe what purports to be their original fighting system.

The proximity of China led to a constant influx of Chinese military techniques which have been used by the Koreans in a characteristic manner.

During the Koryo dynasty (935-1392), martial art training underwent systematic development and a combined system called *soo bakh* was taught to the Korean military. This incorporated weapons training with the sword, spear, and bow, and a close-quarter combat system with knives and grappling. Military games were held annually during May and the eventual victor was promoted. The Yi dynasty extended from 1392 to 1907 and from it, two martial art manuals have survived to the present day.

The Japanese invasion of Korea in 1907 brought the practice of indigenous martial arts to an end and for the next 38 years Koreans were subject to powerful Japanese influences. The Korean military caste was suppressed and its traditions scattered. Later, when Koreans were pressed into becoming co-belligerents, Japanese martial art training was introduced to increase military ardour among officer cadets and conscripts.

Judo, kendo and aikido were well received and replaced the traditions wiped out by the Japanese conquerors. Some karate may also have been introduced at this time. Five martial art academies were set up: Mooduk Kwan, Changmu Kwan, Sungmu Kwan, Jido Kwan and Chungu Kwan, each practising one or more martial arts. During 1964 the government attempted to unify them into the Korean Tae Soo Do Association, which failed because some groups felt they would lose their individual prestige. In the event they were proved correct and those which did join are now almost totally subsumed within the Korean Taekwondo Association, which suc-ceeded the Tae Soo Do Association in 1965.

There are therefore a number of threads within Korea military history. The first is the indigenous tradition, the second comes from Chinese influences and the third from Japanese traditions. There is also a fourth, which is seldom referred to in modern histories, but it is important none the less. This is the recent development which has built on these older elements to produce a uniquely Korean blend. Characteristic features of this blend are most marked in the unarmed combat systems and appear as high, circling kicks and breaking techniques.

Tang soo do is such a latter development. The name translates as 'way of the Chinese (Tang) fist', a title it shared with early Okinawan karate. The Grand Master of this system is Hwang Kee, who during the occupation of Korea escaped into China to avoid being conscripted by the Japanese. While there he practised Chinese martial art, combining it with a pre-existing proficiency in Korean and Japanese traditions. Hwang was one of the dissenters to the Korean government's plans for martial art unification and consequently was refused permission to teach his art outside the country.

TECHNIQUES

Early performances of tang soo do show their mixed origins – high, circling Korean kicks and clear elements of early Shotokan karate producing an interesting blend of

Tang soo do techniques use the full length of the arms and legs to develop maximum power

ing techniques, using a number of pine boards, breeze blocks, or oven-dried bricks.

TRAINING

The class trains in regular lines, wearing the white cotton training tunic called the *tobok*. The jackets are fastened with coloured belts which indicate the stage of attainment of each student. Advancement in competence is measured by a grading system set up according to a syllabus. This requires students to learn a set of techniques appropriate to their skill level. Grades between beginner and black belt are known as *kup* stages. Within the black belt they are called *dan* grades. In some schools, the edges of the jacket may also be trimmed with black.

Basic training

Basic training teaches the individual techniques of tang soo do. Each student practises the appropriate kick or strike while advancing up and down the training hall (*dojang*). Individual techniques are joined together into combinations to teach versatility and flow of movement. Each strike and kick must flow into the next.

Patterns

When the student can combine basic techniques in this fashion, he is ready to begin appreciating pattern practice. Patterns are sequences of combinations designed

technique. Hwang Kee was later allowed to leave Korea and since then, under his personal supervision, tang soo do has changed considerably. Its patterns were previously modelled on karate's but these have been extensively revised.

Tang soo do is pure unarmed combat, using impact techniques, rather than the grappling one would expect to find if traces of early military *soo bakh* origins were present. Strikes fall into what the Chinese would call long-hand boxing, where the full length of the arm is used to generate maximum

power in both straight and circular techniques. The legs are used far more than in the Japanese analogue of karate and the syllabus contains a wider range of kicks. High kicks in particular are favoured but as in taekwondo, there are no foot sweeping or hooking techniques.

Tang soo do is also a hard system, relying on muscular power to develop considerable impact. At the moment of landing, the entire body tightens up with a large muscular contraction that projects maximum force behind the blow. Sometimes this force is demonstrated by break-

Training with a partner teachers the principles of distance, timing and control

Circular kick
1 Bring your kick leg around

2 Raise the knee until it points at the target

3 Straighten your knee and thrust your foot into the target

to improve specific aspects of practice, such as balance and poise. They are also practical, and each move can be shown to have an application with regard to multiple imaginary opponents. However, no matter how sophisticated the pattern, it cannot replace the experience of training with a co-operative partner.

Partner training

Responding to a partner teaches distance and timing: how to remain so close to an opponent that his techniques miss, yet yours are close at hand; when to move, so his attacks are avoided and your response is made before he can recompose or defend himself. These essential skills could be learned within free sparring except that this does not rely on co-operation and there is little opportunity to discuss the merit, or otherwise, of a failed combination.

Pre-arranged sparring

Pre-arranged sparring allows students to train safely yet realistically with combinations. Both attack and

defence are already known; the order of attack is agreed, so the likelihood of injury is low. Both parties proceed at an agreed speed and there is time after each repetition to make a brief assessment of performance. Such feedback is essential to learning.

Free-sparring

Free sparring is confined to skilled tang soo do students. Two students exchange techniques freely but use restricted force and avoid dangerous techniques such as kicks to the groin or open-hand jabs to the eyes. Free sparring is similar in many ways to competition, except insofar as points are awarded for each correct strike or kick to a scoring area of the head and body. Full-power techniques are not permitted because they could result in serious injury.

Circular kicks The techniques of tang soo do are very similar to those of karate and taekwondo but high,

circular kicks are particularly characteristic of it.

Circular kicks use a complicated turning action of the body to change the delivery of the kick into a near horizontal arc. Wherever possible, the foot is raised slightly above target height and then dropped down slightly. This happens even when a kick is aimed at the head. Circular kicks incorporate a large element of accommodation insofar as if the opponent moves onto them, impact force is increased. If he is moving away, they can follow and overtake him.

Either the ball of the foot, the instep or the sole are used to make contact and it is important to be able to form the foot-shape correctly, so your toes and ankles aren't injured. When the instep is used, your toes must all be pointed downwards and the ankle fully stretched, so the shin and instep are as nearly in one straight line as ankle flexibility will allow. If this proves insufficient, you should stretch the joint

4 *Strike with the ball of foot, then snap the foot back and set it down*

3

4

until it will fully extend. The sole of the foot is also used from this position.

When using the ball of the foot the foot is held at a right angle to the shin and all the toes are drawn fully back. Sometimes the little toe curls forwards and if this isn't corrected, a painful injury can result.

All these foot positions must be held lightly yet firmly; tight enough to prevent the foot from wobbling about, yet loose enough not to tie up the muscles of the lower leg.

During circular kicks such as the roundhouse kick, your knee must be raised sufficiently high to the side, in the action known as hip abduction. Limited flexibility of the hips is the major cause of poor circular kicks and must be remedied before effective high kicks can be used. The kicking hip is brought quickly forward to lift over the supporting hip in a smooth, accelerating action. Hesitation or jerkiness will rob the kick of power.

To allow your hips to move as they must, your upper body turns in the direction of the kick, both twisting and leaning back from the target. If this isn't done, your kicking hip can rise only so far and the flight path becomes diagonal instead of horizontal. A diagonal kick can still be effective, though it is more likely to snag on your opponent's elbows or shoulders. Moreover, if hip action is inhibited but the kick allowed to proceed, a powerful twisting force is applied to a normally inflexible joint in the lower back called the sacro-iliac. If this happens too often, the joint becomes inflamed and referred pain occurs in the groin.

As your knee rises to point at the target, the lower leg is driven out by straightening your knee and your foot strikes the target. As your foot approaches your opponent's head, first stop and then reverse the knee action. This snaps your foot out and produces a sharper impact than a straightforward blow would. The whiplash action is extremely fast and makes it difficult for your opponent to seize the spent kick. Natural elasticity in the hamstring muscles spring your foot back and your body resumes its upright position.

At this stage, keeping your balance is most important. Your moving leg has a considerable weight which must be compensated for by moving your upper body. As the kick reaches out your body leans back to avoid loss of balance. As the kick is withdrawn your body returns to a near-upright position, so your foot can be placed down carefully, rather than just dropped heavily.

Reverse circular kick
1 *Twist around and lift the kicking leg*

2 *Begin to straighten the knee joint*

3 *Extend the leg fully as your hips swing you into the target*

3

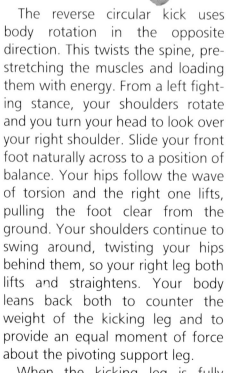

TRAINING AND TACTICS

Reverse turning kick uses body rotation to stretch the muscles in the spine, thereby loading them with power. Move your shoulders first, then allow your hips to follow. The kicking leg accelerates smoothly through the technique, aided by the supporting foot pivoting freely. Keep your eyes on the target at all times and control your centre of gravity. Strike with the sole of your foot.

The reverse circular kick uses body rotation in the opposite direction. This twists the spine, pre-stretching the muscles and loading them with energy. From a left fighting stance, your shoulders rotate and you turn your head to look over your right shoulder. Slide your front foot naturally across to a position of balance. Your hips follow the wave of torsion and the right one lifts, pulling the foot clear from the ground. Your shoulders continue to swing around, twisting your hips behind them, so your right leg both lifts and straightens. Your body leans back both to counter the weight of the kicking leg and to provide an equal moment of force about the pivoting support leg.

When the kicking leg is fully straightened your upper body is leaning right back but your head is raised and your eyes look at the target. Keep your arms close to your sides to prevent them flying out from a guard position. Bend your right knee slightly as the foot approaches the target, so it hooks around and into it. Range is reduced if your knee bends too much.

Circular kicks such as those described above often follow one another in a series. Beginning from a left stance, the right foot is used to deliver a front turning kick to the head. The hips are fully turned as the foot strikes home but it is then not withdrawn close to the body as it would normally be. Instead it is only partially withdrawn and touches down on the ball of the foot. Body rotation continues without hesitation and the left foot next lifts off and curves around into a reverse turning kick.

The angle and distance of the following reverse turning kick can be set precisely by setting down the front turning kick in the appropriate place.

THAI BOXING

HISTORY

The people of Thailand originally came from the Yunnan part of China but during the 13th century were driven south into the Mekong and Salween valleys where they integrated with the native Khmer population. There is little written historical record of these early days and it is not until the Bangkok era of 1767-1932 that records became available.

Early Thai warfare was fought between opposing armies of foot soldiers protected by rhinoceros skin covered shields and helmets. War elephants were used as heavy cavalry to break through massed ranks and during the battle against the Burmese for the northern Thai city

All forms of full contact competition incur the likelihood of brain injury – even when defensive padding is employed

159

THAI BOXING

Young people can train in Thai boxing though they should not take part in competition

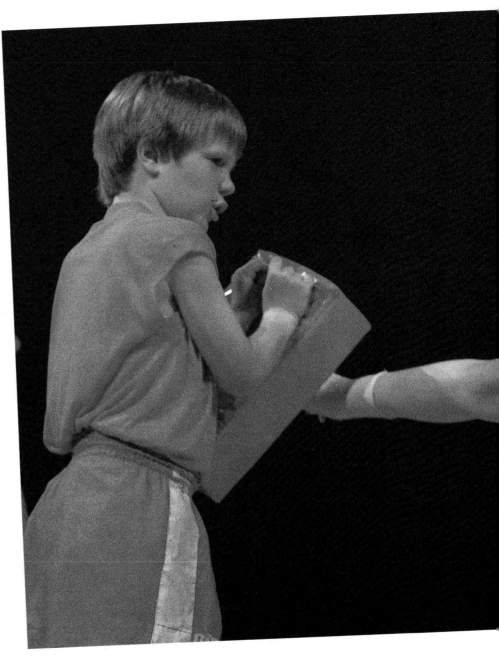

of Chiangmai in 1411, the outcome was settled by a duel between two champions mounted on such beasts.

Firearms were introduced during the 16th century and revolutionised military strategy. Many of the training systems made obsolete by firearms were combined with music to create dances. These are still practised today and the weapons used include the wavy-bladed kris, knives, spears and round shields. The history of many of these ancient dances was destroyed when the Burmese again invaded during 1767.

Nevertheless a form of ritualised combat with ancient weapons, known as krabee-krabong, or sword-spear, has survived. The *krabee* is short and single edged, with a heavy curved blade. The handle is round and ribbed for extra grip, and there is either a small finger guard, or none at all. As the *krabee* is used to slash, the finger guard was probably lost when the weapon became used for ritual rather than military purposes.

Krabee-krabong is practised in pairs, with each combatant carrying a *krabee* and a round shield of woven vegetable fibre. Practice is carefully pre-arranged to minimise injury but the speed and sharpness of the slashing blade make the penalty for error a serious one! Cuts are parried on the shield except when both participants use two swords each. This highly skilled performance presents a whirling, slashing clash of blade against blade as one cut after another rains down

very close to unprotected fingers. As if this weren't dangerous enough, kicks and trips are also used!

Unarmed combat was practised in association with weapon training and one of the greatest exponents was said to be King Naresuan. He was captured by the Burmese in 1560 but was offered his freedom if he could beat the reigning Burmese champion. Naresuan succeeded and from that day, the national sport of

Thai boxing is said to have originated.

During the 18th century Thai boxing flourished in the monasteries where, curiously, it was considered a suitable diversion from the rigours of religious devotion. Matches were violent affairs, with no weight limits and fist bandages spiked with ground glass! If they were feeling fragile, Thai boxers sometimes wore a forearm pad of horsehide or hemp

and the more dangerous blows are prohibited. Until 25 years ago Thai boxing was taught in schools but now it is banned.

Because the competition is so arduous a Thai boxer's career lasts no more than five or six years. Currently 1,500 professional boxers train in the country's many camps, taking the camp's name as their professional surname. Thus it was that Pone Kingpetch, the world flyweight champion in Western boxing, took his surname from the training camp of that name.

Thai boxing is a popular tourist attraction in Thailand, in much the same way that bull-fighting is in Spain. Since the average tourist is hardly an afficionado, the standard of competition is low and features old, injured and tired boxers who no longer have the ability to compete in premier competition and who do not fight with great vigour.

TECHNIQUES

Thai boxing has benefited from studying such systems as karate and taekwondo but this exchange is by no means one way and the Thai circular kicks are now used by many exponents of full contact. Moreover, the president of the French Boxing Federation, Pierre Barruzzy, confirmed that Thai boxing gave rise to the French system of *la savate*.

The striking techniques of Thai boxing resembles those used in other impact-based systems, which is only to be expected as there are limited ways of accelerating the fist and foot into common targets. Thai

but otherwise no protection was permitted. The original rules prohibited biting, grappling, hair pulling and kicking a prone opponent.

Training methods were equally arduous yet surprisingly modern in their approach. Long-distance running developed aerobic stamina while kicking and punching in water improved local muscular endurance in a way closely related to the requirements of boxing technique. Accuracy, speed and timing were

developed by routines such as kicking at a light ball attached by string to a post.

PRESENT-DAY PRACTICE

Thai boxers work out for five or six hours a day and modern training techniques have been incorporated so present-day Thai boxers toughen their shins by pounding them with cola bottles filled with sand! Sparring is restricted to hand techniques

Roundhouse kick
1 *Begin from a left fighting stance, with shoulders relaxed and an effective guard*

boxing does, however, use a highly characteristic form of kick.

Roundhouse kicks

Roundhouse kicks, in which the body rotates around its minor axis, the knee lifts to the side, and the foot travels in a near horizontal arc to the target, feature in many martial arts, but the Thai boxing roundhouse kick is the only one which uses an almost straight leg to deliver the impact.

Begin from a left posture, with your left glove and left foot leading. Throw a right punch and twist your hips behind it, so weight comes off your right foot. Raise your right knee, lifting it out to the side and bringing it forwards across your body while pivoting outwards on your left foot. Your right foot is held relaxed but pointing and your right knee is slightly bent. Your supporting leg continues to pivot until it has turned more than 90 degrees from straight ahead. Your upper body has been pulled around by the action of your shoulders in advancing your right fist and withdrawing the left. Lean your body away from the kick, and from possible counterattacks. Keep both elbows lightly but firmly held to your ribs.

As the kick proceeds, your right knee rises across the front of your body and curves into the target (generally the chin or upper arms), striking it with the shin. If the kick misses, the leg carries on past until it is withdrawn.

The mechanics of the system are worth considering. First of all the kick begins as a twisting action of the spine brought about through turning the shoulders. This stretches the powerful postural muscles of the back and charges them with energy. Secondly, and after a slight lag, the hips turn in behind the shoulders – though they fail to catch the latter up until the kick is virtually complete. The right foot springs up and the slightly bent right knee stretches the muscles on the front of the thigh and lower stomach, so these too are made ready for a strong contraction.

In the second stage, the stretched muscles begin contracting. The spinal muscles drag the kicking hip forward and up. The muscles of the lower stomach and front of thigh accelerate the leg, and the supporting leg turns freely. The effect of this is to apply successively more power as the kick develops.

Roundhouse kicks in other martial arts use extension of the knee joint to drive the foot into the target but this does not occur in Thai boxing. Thai boxers believe that the knee action does not contribute significantly to impact force and by allowing the knee to hinge, much force is in fact lost through recoil. Thai boxing is a full contact activity whereas with the exception of full contact, the other martial arts are not. It may be that the snapping roundhouse kick is ideally suited to a fast delivery of controlled impact. If this is so, then it would be unsuitable for Thai boxing.

The shin is normally a sensitive area, with bone protected by no more than a thin layer of skin. For

this reason, it is necessary to toughen the shin before it can be used extensively. Toughening takes the form of kicking a suspended bag filled with rags, polystyrene packing granules, or sawdust. Continued practice prepares the bone and make it less sensitive to pain, though the process can be disfiguring. Thai boxers under 18 must not follow a rigorous shin-toughening system because of the permanent damage it may cause to developing bones.

2 Swing your right knee forward and up

3 Throw your leg into the target, striking with your shin. Lean back out of harm's way

▼ Ritual headbands
▼ (mongkon) are worn during the pre-fight ritual

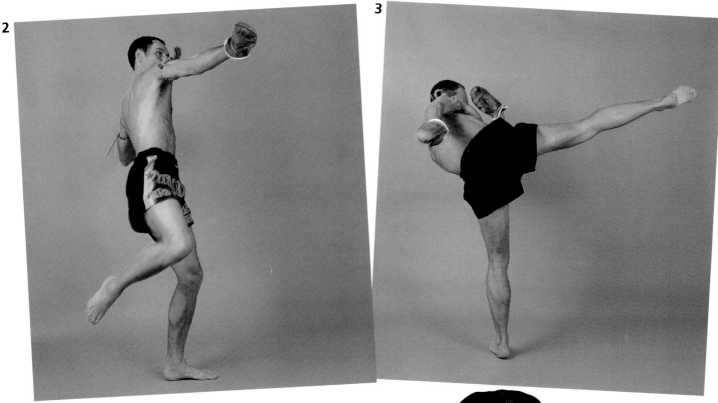

COMPETITIONS

Matches begin with formal ritual where the boxers walk around the ring, holding the top rope. This is said to seal the ring against evil influences. A challenge is issued by a boxer drawing an imaginary line with his toe along the floor of the ring and stamping his foot to challenge his opponent to cross it. Before the match begins each fighter performs a ritual dance known as *ram muay*, the moves of which are symbolic and characteristic of a particular training camp. Thus it is that the boxer performs digging motions, meaning that 'I am here digging your grave!'

Ritual headbands (*mongkon*) are

163

THAI BOXING

Thai boxing competition is perhaps the most violent combat sport of all. No defensive padding is allowed (except for groin guards and boxing gloves) and all blows are full power

*Straight kicks push
the opponent back*

worn by boxers during the ritual but are removed before fighting begins. Discordant music produced by bagpipes and drums serenades the boxers as they psyche themselves up, and during every lull in the fighting.

Uppercuts are seldom used, perhaps because the elbows are considered better weapons in a close-up engagement. Straight kicks are usually delivered off the front leg and push the opponent back. Turning kicks are delivered with the straightened rear leg and make contact with the shin. Knee strikes to the opponent's head are permitted.

The following competition rules are used:

Boxing gloves must weigh be-tween 4 and 6 ounces and be made from leather.

There are 12 weight categories: 112 lb, 118 lb, 122 lb, 126 lb, 130 lb, 135 lb, 141 lb, 147 lb, 150 lb, 160 lb, 175 lb, +175 lb.

The groin must be protected and anklets worn on each leg.

The match comprises five three-minute rounds separated by two-minute rest periods.

The match is judged by a referee in the ring and two judges at the ringside.

Prohibited behaviour includes biting, spitting, striking while holding the ropes, striking a downed opponent and using hip throws or pushes (inner and outer leg reaps are allowed).

GLOSSARY

Bur = Burma, Chi = Chinese, Ind = India, Indo = Indonesia, Jap = Japanese, Kor = Korean, Mal = Malaysia, Phi = Filipino, Tha = Thailand

Age uke (Jap) 'Rising block'; karate deflection of attacks to the head and face.
Age zuki (Jap) 'Rising punch'; karate attack to the jaw or mid-section.
Ai (Jap) 'Harmony'; in aikido the way in which the opponent's force is combined with and so nullified.
Aikido (Jap) 'Way of spirit/harmony'; Japanese martial art which uses the opponent's own force to defeat him, using mainly grappling techniques and body evasions.
Aiki jutsu (Jap) 'Art of spirit/harmony'; predecessor of aikido and a school of jiu jitsu.
Aiuchi (Jap) 'Mutual striking'; each opponent delivering a simultaneous attack.
An marki (Kor) 'Inside block'; taekwondo deflection of attack using the forearm.
Annan sogi (Kor) 'Sitting stance'; taekwondo stance in which the feet are one-and-a-half shoulder widths apart and the knees are equally bent.
An palja sogi (Kor) 'Inner open stance'; taekwondo stance in which the feet are apart and turned slightly inwards.
Anuro marki (Kor) 'Inward block'; taekwondo deflection in which the arm moves from outside the body to the centre.
Anuro taerigi (Kor) 'Inward strike'; taekwondo attack in which the hand strikes from the outside to the body's centre-line.
Ap chagi (Kor) 'Front kick'; thrusting the ball of the foot into the opponent.
Ap cha olligi (Kor) 'Front rising kick'; checking technique using the foot.
Apkumchi (Kor) 'Ball of foot'.
Ap sogi (Kor) 'Front stance'; stance in which 60 per cent of body weight is carried by the front foot.
Armlock Method of applying leverage to the joints of an opponents's arm to cause pain and immobilisation.
Arnis de mano (Phi) 'Usage of hand'; Filipino fighting art which uses the stick, knife and the empty hand.
Ashi barai (Jap) 'Foot sweep'; unbalancing an opponent by striking or hooking his supporting leg.
Ashi garami (Jap) 'Leg entanglement'; trapping an opponent's leg by one's own and applying leverage to it.
Ashi gatami (Jap) 'Leg lock'; locking the opponent's arm using leverage applied by one's foot.
Ashi guruma (Jap) 'Leg wheel'; judo throw in which the opponent is thrown over an extended leg.
Ashi waza (Jap) 'Foot techniques'; all judo techniques which use the leg or foot.
Ate (Jap) 'Strike'; blow delivered by a hand which is not closed into a fist.
Atemi waza (Jap) 'Body strike techniques'; blows and kicks in judo.

Atoshi baraku (Jap) 'A little more time left'; indication of 30 seconds to go in a karate competition bout.
Attention stance Formal stance adopted by martial arts students before beginning training.
Augment Strengthening a technique by harnessing body action to it.
Awasette (Jap) 'Combining together'; adding two half points in competition to produce one full point.
Axe kick Swinging the foot high into the air and then dropping the heel on to the opponent's head or collar bones.
Back fist Punch using the back of the knuckles to attack the side of the head or body.
Back kick Thrusting kick performed with the back turned towards the target. The heel strikes the target.
Baekjul boolgool (Kor) 'Indomitable spirit'.
Bajutsu (Jap) 'Art of horsemanship'.
Bakat marki (Kor) 'Outside block'; deflecting the outside of the opponent's arm or leg.
Bakuro marki (Kor) 'Outward block'; deflection which travels from the body's centre-line out to the side of the body.
Balisong (Phi) Folding dagger.
Balkal (Kor) 'Footsword'; outer edge of the foot below the little toe.
Ball of foot Pad of flesh on the bottom of the foot and exposed when the toes are drawn back.
Bal twikumchi (Kor) 'Heel of foot'.
Bandae chirugi (Kor) 'Reverse punch'; attack using arm opposite the leading foot.
Bandae dollyo chagi (Kor) 'Reverse turning kick'; using a rotational movement of the body to attack an opponent standing to the side, or to the rear.
Bandae dollyo goro (Kor) 'Reverse hooking kick'; turning kick that connects the heel of the kicking foot with the side or back of the opponent's head or body.
Bandal chagi (Kor) 'Crescent kick'; sweeping attack or block which strikes with the foot held vertically. Impact is made with the sole of foot and with the foot edge below the big toe.
Bandal jirugi (Kor) 'Crescent punch'; circular attack with the fist.
Bando (Bur) 'Art of fighting'; Burmese system of armed and unarmed combat.
Ban jayoo daeryon (Kor) 'Semi-free sparring'; training system where both partners know beforehand who will attack and who will defend, and which techniques are to be used.
Baro jirugi (Kor) 'Facing punch'; attack using hand on same side as leading foot.
Basho (Jap) One of the six major 15-day annual sumo tournaments.
Basics Elementary techniques of a martial art, on which all else is built.
Bassai (Jap) 'To Penetrate A Fortress'; *shorin ryu* karate kata.
Batto jutsu (Jap) 'Art of sword cutting'; techniques of drawing the sword and immediately using it to cut down the opponent. Compare with iai-jutsu.
Bear One of the five animals used in the

development of a comprehensive Chinese system of exercises.
Belt Strip of coloured fabric worn around the waist, the colour denoting the wearer's degree of attainment.
Bersilat (Mal) 'To fight'; Malaysian martial art system of armed and unarmed combat.
Bituro chagi (Kor) 'Twisting kick'; kick which curves outwards during its delivery.
Black belt Mark of achievement signifying that the wearer has attained an understanding of a martial art.
Blocking Using the body, arm or leg to interrupt or divert an attack.
Bo (Jap) 'Stave'; wooden staff nearly 2 metres long.
Bogu (Jap) 'Armour'.
Bogu kumite (Jap) 'Sparring in armour'; form of armoured sparring which allows full power strikes and kicks.
Bojutsu (Jap) 'Staff art'; method of using the quarterstaff.
Bokken (Jap) 'Wooden sword'; used in kendo in place of the live blade. Not to be confused with the bamboo shinai, this weapon is made from dense wood.
Breakfall Way of landing safely after falling.
Breaking Method of impact power testing with the body's natural weapons, using wood, tiles, stones and bricks.
Bu (Jap) 'Martial', or 'military'.
Budo (Jap) 'Martial way'; method of practising the martial arts to improve character rather than for battlefield survival.
Budoka (Jap) 'Martial way person'; someone who practises the martial ways.
Bujutsu (Jap) 'Martial art'; fighting arts used by Japanese warriors.
Bunkai (Jap) 'Analysis', method for studying the application of martial art techniques.
Bushi (Jap) 'Warrior'; member of Japan's warrior caste until 15th century, when 'samurai' came to replace it.
Bushido (Jap) 'Way of the warrior'; code of behaviour for the classical Japanese warrior.
Butterfly knife Short, broad-bladed knife used in pairs for kung fu practice.
Chagi (Kor) 'Kicking'.
Cha jirugi (Kor) 'Penetrating kick'.
Chang chuan (Chi) 'Long fist'; northern Chinese style of *wu shu* practised on the mainland.
Chang kwon (Kor) 'Heel of hand'; palm-heel strike.
Chinna (Chi) 'Art of seizing'; Chinese grappling system thought to be the forerunner of jiu jitsu.
Chinto (Jap) 'Fighting towards the East', *shorin ryu* karate kata.
Chirugi (Kor) 'Punch'.
Chi sao (Chi) 'Sticking hands'; method of kung fu training which teaches sensitivity to the opponent's actions.
Choke Grappling technique which stops the opponent from breathing.
Chongul (Kor) 'Front stance'; taekwondo stance in which one foot leads and weight is distributed evenly.

Choy (Chi) One of the five basic schools of shaolin kung fu.

Choy lee fut (Chi) Shaolin style of kung fu using long-arm techniques and many swinging strikes/punches. Founded in 1836 by Chan Heung.

Chuan (Chi) 'Boxing'.

Chuan fa (Chi) 'Way of fist'; general name for Chinese boxing.

Chudan (Jap) 'Middle level'; middle part of the body.

Chudan no-kamae (Jap) 'Middle level guard'; basic position in kendo.

Chudan-tsuki (Jap) 'Middle level strike'; punch to the stomach/chest area.

Chudan uke (Jap) 'Middle level block'; deflection technique against blows and kicks to the stomach/chest level.

Chui (Jap) 'Warning'; admonition given during a competition.

Chukyo marki (Kor) 'Rising block'; deflection technique against descending blows on the head.

Chunin (Jap) 'Middle person'; term of middle rank allegedly applied to ninja.

Chusoki (Jap) 'Ball of foot'.

Circular block Any deflection technique which moves in a circle.

Claw hand Open-hand technique in which the fingers hook.

Combination technique Linking two or more basic techniques into a sequence.

Control Regulation of force used during blows and kicks.

Co-ordination Moving the body and limbs to the correct extent and in the correct sequence.

Crane One of the animals used as a model for schools of kung fu.

Crescent kick Circular kick that sweeps the vertical foot across the front of the body.

Dachi (Jap) 'Position'; posture used during martial art practice.

Daeryon (Kor) 'Sparring'.

Daisho (Jap) 'Big and small'; classical warrior's pair of swords.

Daito (Jap) 'Big blade'; Japanese longsword with blade over 2 feet long.

Dan (Jap) 'Rank'; stage of proficiency within the black belt and sometimes indicated by yellow or gold stripes.

De ashi barai (Jap) 'Advanced foot sweep'; using the foot to hook or knock away the opponent's supporting leg.

Dim mok (Chi) 'Touching vital points'; Chinese method of attacking vulnerable parts of the body by means of a blow or kick.

Do (Jap) 1. 'Way' or 'Path'; philosophical approach to practice. 2. 'Torso'.

Dobok (Kor) 'Uniform'; martial art training tunic'.

Dogi (Jap) 'Martial way uniform'; tunic worn for practice.

Dojang (Kor) 'Place of training'.

Dojo (Jap) 'Place of training in the way'; traditional training hall.

Dollyo chagi (Kor) 'Turning kick'; kicking in a horizontal arc into the target.

Dollyo jirugi (Kor) 'Turning punch'; blow which travels in a circular fashion.

Drunken style Sequence found in some kung fu styles in which the practitioner behaves as though drunk.

Duro marki (Kor) 'Scooping block'; deflection technique against kicks.

Dwi chagi (Kor) 'Back kick'.

Dwit bal sogi (Kor) 'Rear foot stance'; stance in which most of the body weight is brought back over the rear foot and the heel of the leading foot lifts from the floor.

Dwitcha jirugi (Kor) 'Back penetrating kick'; thrusting back kick using the heel.

Empi uchi (Jap) 'Elbow strike'; short-range technique used to attack the ribs, sternum, jaw and head.

Encho-sen (Jap) 'Continuation'; extension to a karate bout in which the first to score wins.

Enpi (Jap) 'Swallow'; *shorin ryu* karate kata.

Escrima (Phi) Another name for Arnis de mano.

External system Any Chinese fighting system which stresses the importance of muscular power.

Five animals The tiger, bear, monkey, deer and bird, whose movements served as the basis for a system of exercises.

Flying kick Kick delivered when both feet are clear of the floor.

Focus Concentration of impact force.

Forearm block Deflection technique using the arm between the wrist and the elbow.

Form 1. Expression of style. 2. Sequence of techniques performed in a pre-arranged order, direction and speed.

Forward stance Basic stance in which the hips are turned to face the front, the front knee is bent and the rear knee is straightened.

Freestyle sparring Most advanced form of sparring in which unprogrammed techniques are exchanged. Control is used to minimise injury.

Front kick Attack in which the knee rises to the front and the kick is thrust or snapped out, striking with the ball of foot.

Fudo dachi (Jap) 'Immovable stance'; karate stance in which both knees are bent as in a straddle stance but weight is brought more over the leading foot and the hips are turned forward-facing.

Fugul (Kor) 'Back stance'; stance in which 70 per cent of body weight is borne by the rear foot.

Full contact Fighting system in which full power techniques are used to knock the opponent out.

Fumikomi (Jap) 'Step in'; stamping kick to the opponent's knee, shin, or instep.

Gankaku (Jap) 'Crane on a rock'; *shorin ryu* kata.

Garami (Jap) 'Entanglement'.

Gari (Jap) Reaping action to the opponent's supporting leg.

Gatame (Jap) 'Locking', or 'holding'.

Gedan barai (Jap) 'Downward parry'; forearm deflection sweep against attacks to the lower stomach and groin.

Gedan tsuki (Jap) 'Downward strike'; punch to lower stomach and groin area.

Genin (Jap) 'Low person'; ordinary ninja.

Geri (Jap) 'Kick'.

Gi (Jap) 'Uniform'; martial art training tunic.

Gohon kumite (Jap) 'Five-step sparring'; five consecutive and identical attacks, each with the same response. A counterattack is also performed in response to the fifth.

Goju ryu (Jap) 'Hard/soft tradition'; style of karate based on *shorei ryu* and founded by Kannryo Higaonna.

Goju shiho (Jap) 'Fifty-four steps', *shorin ryu* karate kata.

Goman (Kor) 'End'; command given to stop practice.

Goro chagi (Kor) 'Sweeping kick'; hooking or jarring the opponent's supporting leg, causing him to fall or stagger.

Goshi (Jap) 'Hip'.

Goshin jutsu (Jap) 'Self-defence art'; practical techniques of self-defence.

Goyangee sogi (Kor) 'Cat stance'; stance in which 90 per cent of body weight is carried over the rear leg.

Grappling techniques Fighting systems which use locks, holds and throws to defeat the opponent.

Groundwork Judo techniques applied when both parties are on the ground.

Guard Positioning the body, arms and legs to allow maximum use of body weapons while reducing the target opportunities for the opponent.

Gungul sogi (Kor) 'Walking stance'; high posture with one foot leading the other.

Gup (Kor) 'Grade'; rank below black belt.

Gyaku mawashigeri (Jap) 'Reverse roundhouse kick'; turning kick which strikes with the heel, or the sole of the foot.

Gyaku tsuki (Jap) 'Reverse punch'; punch performed with the opposite fist to the leading leg.

Hachimaki (Jap) 'Head wrapping'; cotton towel around the forehead to keep sweat from the eyes.

Haishu (Jap) 'Back of hand'.

Haisoku (Jap) 'Instep'.

Haito (Jap) 'Ridge hand'; thumb-side edge of the hand used in circular strikes.

Hajime (Jap) 'Begin'; command to begin sparring.

Hakama (Jap) 'Split skirt'; loose flowing over-trousers.

Haktari seogi (Kor) 'Crane stance'; one-legged posture with the lifted foot placed on the supporting knee.

Hammer fist Blow with the little-finger edge of the fist.

Hanare (Jap) Point in Japanese archery at which the arrow is released.

Hanbo (Jap) 'Short stick'; truncheon.

Hane goshi (Jap) 'Spring hip throw'; judo throwing technique using the bent leg to lift the opponent.

Hane makikomi (Jap) 'Outer winding spring hip throw'; judo throwing technique.

Hangetsu (Jap) 'Half moon'; *shorei ryu* karate kata.

Hangetsu dachi (Jap) 'Half moon stance'; very strong stance in which the muscles are tensed against each other. The feet are turned inwards and the heel of the front foot is in line with the toes of the following foot.

Hanmei (Jap) 'Half body'; posture in which the body is turned slightly away from direct forwards-facing.

Hanshi (Jap) 'Master'; very senior grade of at least eighth dan.

Hansoku (Jap) 'Foul'.

Hantei (Jap) 'Decision'; of judging panel in a match.

Hapkido (Kor) 'Way of spirit/body harmony'; Korean equivalent of aikido, though the former also includes a wide variety of striking techniques.

Hara (Jap) 'Abdomen'.

Harai goshi (Jap) 'Sweeping hip throw'; judo technique to lever the opponent over while sweeping his supporting leg.

Hara kiri (Jap) 'Belly slitting'; informal term for Japanese ritual suicide.

Hardan (Kor) 'Low level'; groin and lower stomach area.

Heel kick Kick which uses the heel to strike the opponent.

Heian (Jap) 'Peace'; series of five karate katas originated by Yasutsune Itosu.

Hidari (Jap) 'Left'.

Hiji (Jap) 'Elbow'; alternative word for Empi.

Hikiwake (Jap) 'Draw'; verdict in a tied match.

Hiraken (Jap) 'Flat fist'; fist in which the fingertips press against the top of the palm but the fist doesn't close fully.

Hiza (Jap) 'Knee'.

Hiza guruma (Jap) 'Knee wheel'; judo technique which throws the opponent with a circular motion.

Hojo jutsu (Jap) 'Art of tying'; part of the warrior's training and used to immobilise a captive.

Hojutsu (Jap) 'Art of firearms'.

Hold Immobilising technique.

Hold down Technique applied during groundwork to immobilise the opponent and prevent him from rising.

Honbu (Jap) 'Headquarters'; martial art school or tradition's main base.

Hop gar (Chi) Kung fu style most noted for its footwork and practical application.

Horse stance Stance in which the feet are wide apart, the knees bend equally and the back is straight.

Hourglass stance Stable stance in which the heel of the leading foot is in line with the toes of the following foot. The feet are turned inwards.

Hsing-I (Chi) Form of kung fu which does not use great muscular power and which relies on linear movements.

Hung gar (Chi) Prominent style of southern shaolin kung fu, believed to be an ancestor of karate.

Hwarang do (Kor) 'Way of the flowering youth'; code of ethics of a group of elite Korean warriors known as the Hwa Rang.

Hyung (Kor) Series of techniques performed in order, at a set speed and in set directions.

Iaido (Jap) 'Way of the sword'; drawing, using

and returning of the Japanese sword.

Iai jutsu (Jap) 'Sword art'; practical tradition of drawing, cutting with and re-sheathing the sword.

Ibuki (Jap) 'Breath control'; method of breathing in which air is noisily forced out.

Inner block Block in which the forearm sweeps from the outside of the body to the inside.

Internal system Kung fu system in which power is not generated by obvious muscular action.

Ippon (Jap) 'One point'; full scoring point in a competition.

Ippon ken (Jap) 'One knuckle fist'; natural body weapon in which the index or middle finger knuckle is extruded.

Ippon seoi nage (Jap) 'One-arm shoulder throw'; judo technique.

Ippon shobu (Jap) 'One point throw'; competition decided by a single full point.

Jigo hontai (Jap) Judo defensive posture with both knees bent and the hips lowered, making it difficult to throw.

Jikan (Jap) 'Time'; announcement when the clock is stopped during a match.

Jion (Jap) Shorei ryu karate kata named after the famous Buddhist temple at Jion-ji.

Jirugi (Kor) 'Punch'.

Jitte (Jap) 'Ten hands'; shorei ryu karate kata.

Jiu ippon kumite (Jap) 'One point semi-free sparring'; karate training system in which the attacking technique is pre-arranged but the opponent can respond as he chooses.

Jiu jitsu (Jap) 'Compliant art'; system of grappling without meeting force with force.

Jiu kumite (Jap) 'Free sparring'; training system in which techniques can be exchanged but a measure of control is retained.

Jo (Jap) 'Stave'; heavy stick used singly or as a pair.

Jodan (Jap) 'Upward'; shoulders, neck and head areas.

Jodan uke (Jap) 'Upward block'; deflection which sweeps the shoulders and head clear of attacking techniques.

Jogai (Jap) 'Out of bounds'; stepping out of the match area.

Jojutsu (Jap) 'Stave art'; techniques of using the jo.

Jonin (Jap) Experienced ninja.

Joomuk (Kor) 'Fist'.

Judo (Jap) 'Compliant way'; jiu jitsu school refined by Jigoro Kano into an Olympic combat sport.

Judogi (Jap) 'Judo uniform'; tunic worn during judo practice.

Judoka (Jap) 'Judo person'; someone who practises judo.

Juji gatame (Jap) 'Cross armlock'; elbow lock that levers the captured and extended arm against the thigh.

Juji jime (Jap) 'Cross lock'; choke hold applied from a cross-grip of the opponent's collar.

Juji uke (Jap) 'Cross block' or 'x-block'; deflecting attacks between the crossed forearms.

Junbi sogi (Kor) 'Ready stance'; formal stance used before actual practice begins.

Jutsu (Jap) 'Art'; used after the martial art name shows that the tradition is based on true military practice.

Jutte (Jap) Forked iron truncheon.

Kakato (Jap) 'Heel'.

Kakato geri (Jap) 'Heel kick'.

Kalaripayat (Ind) Indian fighting art using daggers, the staff and unarmed combat.

Kama (Jap) 'Sickle'; covert weapon used by Okinawan karateka.

Kamae (Jap) 'Stance'; posture adopted during martial art practice.

Kami basani (Jap) 'Crab scissors'; sacrifice throw using the legs.

Kancho (Jap) 'Grand master'; chief instructor of a karate school or style.

Kanku (Jap) 'Looking to the sky'; shorin karate kata.

Kansetsu waza (Jap) 'Locking techniques'; techniques which immobilise the joints by means of leverage.

Karate (Jap) 'China hand' and later 'Empty hand'; Okinawan fighting system transported to Japan where it was refined in a martial way. The meaning of the name changed at that time.

Karate do (Jap) 'Way of karate'; study of karate for sporting or character-building reasons.

Karategi (Jap) 'Karate uniform'; tunic worn for practice.

Karate jutsu (Jap) 'Art of karate'; study of karate for practical purposes.

Karateka (Jap) 'Karate person'; someone who practises karate.

Kata (Jap) 'Formal exercise'; pre-arranged sequence of techniques performed at a set speed and in set directions. See also 'form' and 'hyung'.

Kata gatame (Jap) 'Shoulder hold'; joint-immobilising lock using an arm to apply leverage.

Kata guruma (Jap) 'Shoulder wheel'; judo throw in which the opponent is first lifted to the shoulders and then thrown.

Katana (Jap) 'Sword'; single-edged, curved Japanese sword.

Keage (Jap) 'Kicking up'; kick that swings up to the target.

Keibo (Jap) Wooden truncheon.

Keiko (Jap) 'Chicken's beak'; strike using the pursed fingers.

Keikogu (Jap) Half-point penalty in a karate match.

Kekomi (Jap) 'Thrust'.

Kempo (Jap) Japanese rendering of the Chinese word 'chuan fa'.

Kendo (Jap) 'Way of the Sword'; combat sport which uses armour and the bamboo shinai.

Kendoka (Jap) 'Kendo person'; someone who practises kendo.

Ken jutsu (Jap) 'Sword art'; techniques of practical swordsmanship used by Japanese warriors on the battlefield.

Kenshi (Jap) 'Fencer'.

Keri waza (Jap) 'Kicking techniques'.

Kesa gatame (Jap) 'Scarf hold'; judo technique applied across the opponent's neck.

Ki (Jap) 'Spirit'; energy form produced by the body and harnessed by certain martial arts.

Kiai (Jap) 'Spirit harmony'; joining of the will to body action and expressed as a loud shout.

Kibadachi (Jap) 'Straddle stance'; form of horse stance in which the feet are parallel or converging.

Kick boxing Another name for Full contact.

Kihon (Jap) 'Basics'; fundamental techniques of martial art practice.

Kime (Jap) 'Focus'; concentration of power at a certain point during a technique.

Kiritsu (Jap) 'Stand'; instruction to return a class to their feet after a kneeling salutation ritual.

Kobudo (Jap) 'Old martial way'; practice of classical budo systems.

Kobujutsu (Jap) 'Old martial art'; practice of old martial arts.

Kodachi (Jap) 'Small sword'; shorter sword of the pair worn by the Japanese warrior, known collectively as the Daisho.

Kodokan (Jap) 'Hall for teaching the way'; training centre for judo established by the founder, Jigoro Kano, in 1882.

Kogusoku (Jap) One predecessor of jiu jitsu.

Kohai (Jap) Class junior.

Kokutsu dachi (Jap) 'Back stance'; stance in which 70 per cent of body weight is moved over the rear foot.

Koshi (Jap) 'Ball of foot', or 'hip'.

Koshi waza (Jap) 'Hip techniques'; throwing techniques which use the hips.

Kote (Jap) 'Wrist'; thick protective gauntlets worn by kendoka.

Kote waza (Jap) 'Wrist locking techniques'; judo techniques.

Krabee Krabong (Tha) Thai fighting system using a pair of short swords, or a short sword and a shield.

Kung fu (Chi) 'Well done'; common name for schools of Chinese martial art practised outside the Chinese mainland.

Kuoshu (Chi) 'National art'; now replaced by Wu shu.

Kup (Kor) Alternative spelling of Gup.

Kusarigama (Jap) 'Chain and sickle'; compound specialist weapon used by warrior monks.

Ku shanku (Jap) Chinese military attache to Okinawa who taught a karate kata.

Kwanku (Jap) Alternative and older spelling of Kanku.

Kwoon (Chi) 'Training hall'.

Kyochka marki (Kor) 'Cross block'; deflection in which the forearms cross over, also known as 'x-block'.

Kyokushinkai (Jap) 'Way of ultimate truth association'; karate school founded by the Korean, Masutatsu Oyama.

Kyoshi (Jap) 'Teacher grade'; at least a 6th dan grade of instructor.

Kyu (Jap) 'Grade'; levels below black belt.

Kyudo (Jap) 'Way of the bow'; martial way based on kyu jutsu. .

Kyu jutsu (Jap) 'Art of the bow'; techniques of archery in the battlefield.

Lathi (Ind) 'Stick'; Indian stick fighting art that uses a 5-foot bamboo stave.

Law horn kuen (Chi) Kung fu style known for its high kicks.

Lock Technique that immobilises a joint by applying leverage across it.

Long-hand boxing Schools of Chinese martial art which use punches relying on full elbow extension.

Lunge punch Advancing punch normally delivered from a forward stance.

Maai (Jap) 'Distancing'; distance between two opponents.

Maegeri (Jap) 'Front kick'.

Mae tobigeri (Jap) 'Front flying kick'; jumping front kick delivered with both feet off the ground.

Maki komi (Jap) 'Winding'; action used in judo throws to lever the opponent over.

Makiwara (Jap) 'Straw padded post'; training aid for the fist.

Manriki gusari (Jap) 'Ten thousand power chain'; chain weighted at either end and used as a weapon.

Marki (Kor) 'Block'; defensive action which interrupts or deflects an attack.

Martial arts Military techniques, or those techniques used by the classical warrior.

Mawashigeri (Jap) 'Roundhouse kick'; kick in which the foot travels in a horizontal arc to the target.

Mawashi tsuki (Jap) 'Roundhouse punch'; punch in which the fist travels in a horizontal arc to the target.

Meijin (Jap) 'Expert'; highly skilled martial artist who has gone beyond technique itself and transformed his techniques into what amounts to an art form.

Men (Jap) Head protector used in kendo. It has a steel face grille and can withstand a heavy impact.

Migi (Jap) 'Right' (cf. hidari).

Mizu no kokoro (Jap) 'Mind like water'; principle of Buddhist meditation which calms the mind.

Moa sogi (Kor) 'Close stance'; ritual stance in which the feet are brought close together.

Mokuso (Jap) 'Quiet thought'; pause for meditation preceding or following training.

Monkey One of the five animals on which a system of kung fu exercises is based.

Monkey style Kung fu school which bases its training on the actions of the monkey.

Mooreup (Kor) 'Knee'.

Morote tsuki (Jap) 'Double punch'; delivering a blow simultaneously with both fists.

Morote uke (Jap) 'Double block'; using both arms to increase the effectiveness of a block.

Mo seogi (Kor) 'Ready for action', stance in which the feet are separated and one leads the other.

Motonoichi (Jap) 'Return to original position'; direction for contestants in competitions.

Muay Thai (Tha) Thai boxing, a form of full contact, using boxing gloves and developed in Thailand.

Musubi dachi (Jap) 'Informal attention stance'; stance in which the heels are together but the feet turn outwards.

Nagashi tsuki (Jap) 'Flowing punch'; snap punch performed at an angle to the opponent.

Nage waza (Jap) 'Throwing techniques'; techniques in which the opponent is unbalanced and thrown to the floor.

Naginata (Jap) 'Reaping sword'; halberd with a sword blade attached to a long handle.

Naginata do (Jap) 'Way of using the reaping sword'; method of practice based on using the naginata.

Naginata jutsu (Jap) 'Art of using the reaping sword'; military use of the naginata.

Naha te (Jap) 'Hand of Naha'; one of the three early forms of classic Okinawan karate.

Naihanchi (Jap) Karate kata named after a Chinese military attache in Okinawa.

Najunde (Kor) 'Low'; lower stomach and groin region.

Narani sogi (Kor) 'Parallel stance'; formal posture in which the feet are a shoulder width apart and parallel.

Nei chia (Chi) Internal school of kung fu which places no great emphasis on muscular effort.

Nekoashi dachi (Jap) 'Cat stance'; stance in which most of the body weight is borne by the rear leg, the front foot just resting lightly.

Ne waza (Jap) 'Ground techniques'; judo groundwork techniques.

Ninja (Jap) 'Stealer in'; hired spy or assassin.

Nippon kempo (Jap) 'Japanese boxing'; martial art which uses a kendo type protective helmet, breastplate and boxing gloves.

Nopunde marki (Kor) 'High block'; deflection which sweeps the shoulders and head clear of attack.

Northern styles Family of kung fu systems characterised by large movements and many kicks. cf Southern styles.

Nukite (Jap) 'Spear hand'; thrusting the fingers of the extended hand into the opponent.

Nunchaku (Jap) 'Wooden flail'; weapon made from two wooden batons linked by a chain or thong.

Odachi (Jap) 'Great sword'; weapon worn together with the kodachi by Japanese warriors.

Ogoshi (Jap) 'Major hip throw'; judo technique in which the opponent is levered over the hip.

Oguruma (Jap) 'Major wheel'; judo throw over the extended leg.

Oi tsuki (Jap) 'Lunge punch'.

Okinawa te (Jap) 'Hand of Okinawa'; all Okinawan karate.

One knuckle fist Fist in which the middle joint of the index or middle finger leads the others.

One-step sparring Karate training system in which the attacker performs a single, pre-arranged attack and the defender responds in an agreed manner.

Orun (Kor) 'Right'.

Osae waza (Jap) 'Holding techniques'; immobilising methods during judo groundwork.

O-sensei (Jap) 'Great teacher'; usually the founder of a tradition, or its chief instructor.

O soto gari (Jap) 'Major outer reap'; judo throw which combines an unbalancing push with hooking the supporting leg.

Otoshi (Jap) 'Drop'.

Outside block Forearm block which sweeps from

the inside to the outside of the body.

Pak mei 'White eyebrows'; kung fu style named after the originator's nickname.

Pa kua 'Eight trigrams'; one of the three internal schools of kung fu.

Palmheel Thrusting strike with the heel of the hand.

Parro (Kor) 'Return'; pulling back to a basic stance after training.

Parry Deflecting a blow or kick.

Pattern See 'form', or 'kata'.

Peh hoke (Chi) 'White crane'; kung fu style characterised by evasion and counterattack.

Penjak silat (Indo) National martial art of Indonesia, using both armed and unarmed combat.

Pinan (Jap) 'Peaceful mind'; analogous to the five heian katas and devised in 1903 by Yasutsune Itosu.

Poomse (Kor) See 'Hyung'.

Praying mantis Kung fu style characterised by strong arm movements.

Pre-arranged sparring Pair-form sparring in which both the attack and defence are determined beforehand.

Quan Tao (Chi) Heavy halberd-like weapon.

Randori (Jap) 'Free exercise'; free sparring in judo.

Rank Level of proficiency attained.

Reap Taking the opponent's supporting leg away in judo.

Rei (Jap) 'Bow'.

Renraku waza (Jap) 'Combination techniques'; linking basic techniques together in a sequence.

Renshi (Jap) 'Accomplished person'; normally fifth or sixth dans.

Renshu (Jap) 'Practice'.

Reverse punch Punch delivered with the opposite fist to the leading leg.

Reverse roundhouse kick Kick delivered with the heel or sole of foot travelling in a horizontal arc.

Ridge hand Circular strike using the thumb-side of the hand edge.

Rohei (Jap) *Shorin ryu* karate kata.

Rokushakubo (Jap) 'Six-foot staff'.

Roundhouse kick Kick delivered with the instep or ball of foot travelling in a horizontal arc.

Roundhouse punch Punch that travels along a circular path.

Ryu (Jap) 'Tradition'; core of teachings which separate one school from another.

Sabom (Kor) 'Teacher'.

Sacrifice throws Judo throws in which one is prepared to fall in the process of throwing the opponent.

Sai (Jap) Short-handled and heavy trident which can also serve as a truncheon.

Sambo daeryon (Kor) 'Three-step sparring'; training system in which the attacker advances with three identical and consecutive attacks as the defender steps back and blocks. The final attack is followed by a counter-attack.

Samurai (Jap) 'One who serves'; title of the Japanese warrior caste.

Sanbon kumite (Jap) 'Three-step sparring'.

Sanchin (Jap) Karate kata devised by Chojun Miyagi of the Goju ryu.

Sanchin dachi (Jap) 'Hourglass stance'.

Sankaku-jime (Jap) 'Triangular necklock'; immobilising technique in which the opponent is held by his neck and one of his arms.

Seiken (Jap) 'Forefist'.

Seisan (Jap) Karate kata named after its originator.

Seiza (Jap) 'Correct sitting'; formal kneeling position.

Sempai (Jap) 'Senior'; next senior grade in the training hall below the instructor.

Sensei (Jap) 'Teacher'.

Seoi nage (Jap) 'Shoulder throw'; judo technique.

Seppuku (Jap) Formal name for ritual suicide.

Set Used interchangeably with 'pattern'.

Shaolin (Chi) Famous Buddhist monastery associated with martial art practice. It is still in existence, in a rebuilt form.

Shejak (Kor) 'Begin'; command to start training.

Shiai jo (Jap) 'Contest place'; where competitions are held.

Shihan (Jap) 'Supreme teacher'; of a school or tradition.

Shiko dachi (Jap) Modified horse stance with the feet turned outwards.

Shime waza (Jap) 'Strangulation techniques'; judo chokes and strangles.

Shimpan (Jap) 'Referee'.

Shito ryu (Jap) Karate school founded by Kenwa Mabuni.

Shizentai (Jap) 'Natural position'; relaxed yet attentive stance in which one foot slightly leads the other.

Shorei ryu (Jap) Okinawan karate style developed from naha-te.

Shorinji kempo (Jap) 'Shaolin Temple Boxing'; Japanese rendering of shaolin kung fu.

Shorin ryu (Jap) Okinawan style founded on the older school of *shuri te*.

Shotokan (Jap) 'Shoto's club'; Gichin Funakoshi's Japanese honbu.

Shuai chiao (Chi) Form of Chinese wrestling.

Shugyo (Jap) 'Intense training'.

Shukokai (Jap) 'Way for all'; offshoot of Mabuni's *shito ryu* founded by the latter's student, Chojiro Tani.

Shuriken (Jap) Sharp-edged throwing star.

Shuri te (Jap) One of the earliest recognisable Okinawan karate styles, from which came *shorin ryu*.

Shuto (Jap) 'Knife hand'; little finger edge of the hand.

Side kick Kick using the heel and edge of foot and driven out while the body is turned sideways-on to the opponent.

Sifu (Chi) 'Teacher'.

Silat (Indo) 'Fast action'; Indonesian martial arts; some armed, some unarmed.

Siu lum (Chi) Cantonese rendering of Shaolin.

Snap kick Kick that is smartly retrieved after use.

Sogi (Kor) 'Stance'.

So jutsu (Jap) 'Spear art'; practical techniques of spear-usage.

Sokuto (Jap) 'Knife foot'; little toe edge of the foot.

Soto uke (Jap) 'Outside block'; deflection in which the forearm moves from the centre of the body to the outside.

Southern styles Kung fu schools characterised by strong stances and few kicks.

Sparring Exchange of techniques with a partner.

Spear hand Hand weapon which thrusts the extended fingers into the target.

Staff Wooden pole about 6 feet long.

Stamping kick Kick which drives the heel downward into the target.

Stance Posture in which body weight is poised and stable.

Sticking hands Form of sparring practice in Wing Chun kung fu, which relies on feeling the opponent's intent and responding.

Straddle stance Another name for horse stance.

Style Particular rendering of a martial way or martial art based on an individual interpretation.

Suiei jutsu (Jap) 'Swimming art'; used by classical warriors.

Sumo (Jap) Japanese wrestling in which the object is either to make the opponent touch the ground with anything other than the soles of his feet, or to thrust/throw him out of the area.

Sutemi waza (Jap) 'Sacrifice techniques'.

Sweep Displacing the opponent's supporting foot by a hook or strike, so he loses balance.

Tachi (Jap) Earlier Japanese longsword worn with the cutting edge facing downwards, replaced by the katana circa 1600.

Taekwondo (Kor) 'Kick/punch way'; martial arts of Korea, now developing a single, common identity.

Tai Chi Chuan (Chi) Cantonese reading of 'Great ultimate fist', one of the three internal Chinese martial arts.

Taiho jutsu (Jap) 'Arrest techniques'; police methods as the basis of a self-defence system.

Tai jutsu (Jap) 'Body art'; predecessor of jiu jitsu.

Tai otoshi (Jap) 'Body drop'; judo throw which takes the opponent over a straightened leg.

Tai sabaki (Jap) 'Body movement'; evasion techniques to make an attack miss.

Tameshiwari (Jap) 'To test by breaking'; method of testing the impact power of a technique by using wood, tiles and bricks.

Tanden (Jap) 'Abdomen'; centre of gravity.

Tang soo do (Kor) 'Way of the Tang hand'; fighting system strongly influenced by karate but now pursuing its own line of development.

Tan tien (Chi) Equivalent to 'Tanden'; area in which chi energy is generated.

Tanto (Jap) Single-edged dagger.

Tatami (Jap) 'Mat'.

Te (Jap) 'Hand'; early Okinawan karate.

Teisoku (Jap) 'Sole of foot'.

Tekki (Jap) 'Horse riding'; set of three katas derived from Naihanchi.

Tensyo (Jap) Training kata devised by *Goju ryu* karate founder Chojun Miyagi.

Thai boxing See 'Muay Thai'.

Tomari te (Jap) One of the three older schools of Okinawan karate, later subsumed into *shuri te*.

Tomoe nage (Jap) 'Circle throw'; judo sacrifice throw which plants a foot in the opponent's stomach and wheels him over.

Tonfa (Jap) 'Handle'; Okinawan covert weapon used in karate practice.

Tori (Jap) 'Taker'; the one who performs a technique on his partner.

To te (Jap) 'Tang hand'; early name for Okinawan karate.

Tsuki (Jap) 'Thrust'; any sharp pushing action.

Tsuki waza (Jap) 'Punching techniques'.

Tsuzukete (Jap) 'Continue'; command given by the referee.

Uchi (Jap) 'Strike'; technique delivered with the hand partially or fully open.

Uchimata (Jap) 'Inner thigh throw'; judo throwing technique that uses the power of a lifting foot to throw the opponent.

Ude (Jap) 'Forearm'.

Ude garami (Jap) 'Entangled armlock'; judo lock that works against the elbow joint.

Ude uke (Jap) 'Forearm block'.

Uechi ryu (Jap) Style of Okinawan karate founded by Kanbun Uechi.

Uke (Jap) 1. Block. 2. Person who receives tori's technique.

Ukemi (Jap) 'Art of falling'; judo techniques of falling safely.

Upward block Deflection technique that travels upwards.

Uraken (Jap) 'Reverse fist'; striking with the back of the two large knuckles.

Ushiro geri (Jap) 'Back kick'; thrusting kick directly behind that strikes with the heel of the foot.

Vajramushti (Ind) Early Indian martial art of which almost no trace can now be found.

Wa (Jap) 'Harmony'.

Wado ryu (Jap) 'Way of harmony tradition'; karate style founded by Hironori Ohtsuka.

Wakizashi (Jap) 'Short sword'; weapon worn with the katana.

Waza (Jap) 'Technique'.

Waza ari (Jap) 'Half point'; score for a slightly imperfect technique.

Wei chia (Chi) 'External system'; kung fu forms which use a great deal of muscular effort.

Wing chun (Chi) Style of southern kung fu devised by the Buddhist nun Ng Mui.

Wu shu (Chi) 'Martial art'; martial arts of the Chinese mainland.

X-block Blocking an attack with crossed forearms.

Yaksok daeryon (Kor) 'Pre-arranged sparring'.

Yama zuki (Jap) 'Combined punch'; thrusting both arms out together.

Yamei (Jap) 'Halt!'; command to stop training.

Yari (Jap) 'Spear'.

Yaup choomuk (Kor) 'Hammer fist'.

Yikwon (Kor) 'Back fist'.

Yoko geri (Jap) 'Side kick'.

Yop chagi (Kor) 'Side kick'.

Yudansha (Jap) 'Black belt holder'.

Zanshin (Jap) 'Alert posture'; maintaining alertness to an opponent's capabilities.

Zen (Jap) Buddhist sect often associated with martial art practice.

Zenkutsudachi (Jap) 'Forward stance'; basic posture used in karate.

INDEX